His Guiding Hand

Bill Richens

I would like to acknowledge the invaluable help and support from my daughter-in-law-Antonia-- for her cover illustration and her help in putting my story together- Thank you Toni--

His Guiding Hand
Copyright © 2020 by Bill Richens

Tellwell Talent
www.tellwell.ca

ISBN
978-0-2288-2760-3 (Paperback)

I wrote this book to convey to the reader that the many seemingly unimportant events that cross our path as we travel this journey through life often have a deeper meaning and a definite purpose further along life's road. The reader may judge for themselves and form their own conclusions. It may be difficult for many to attribute these things to an all knowing God, narrow escapes are often written off as 'luck', this word has no credibility in my vocabulary, my only regret being not to have 'found' Him earlier in life, but then, it is written that He knew me while I was yet in my mother's womb

--Bill Richens

"HIS GUIDING HAND" An account of the life of the Author, Bill Richens, born in the south of England, in 1932, the early years of boyhood, the normal life of a mischievous boy who loved the green fields, the rivers and woods of that part of the country, the slow realization that the things that happened during his many adventures were not the product of mere chance or co-incidence. Later on in the book and far away in another country, the events that brought him to recognise the Hand of God in his life

---

"I am sorry Bill, I can only give your Mother a week to live." As I sat in the doctor's office, his words were lost in the dreadful cold feeling that came down it seemed upon my very soul, he went on to say, "Your mother was admitted with what was previously diagnosed as a simple lung congestion, further tests have revealed an advanced cancerous condition that is untreatable, her entire body is infected with the disease, if only she had come in earlier there would have been a hope for her survival, now there is none". He went on to say that because Mom had been a nurse, back in England, she surely knew the early symptoms of the disease, I left the office in despair, on the verge of tears, only one who has experienced a situation similar to this can understand, I drove up to a lonely quiet graveyard to sit, just to be alone, and this, later on in the book, is where my story really starts..

Chapter One

The Sixth of September, 1932, was a fairly uneventful day, at least as far as the rest of the world was concerned. The great depression had the United States in its relentless grip, hungry men rode the rails looking for work, but for me it was a special day that deserved a mark on the calendar, it was the day that I arrived on planet Earth. My poor mother had a very hard delivery, or so my sister Joan informed me many years later. Mom watched as the midwife placed me in a convenient cardboard box, then she turned to Mom and said, 'I am sorry but your baby boy is dead!'

My mother was too sick to show much emotion as the nurse went through the legal procedure of calling the resident doctor to make the final examination of the body and sign the death certificate. Back in those days, in the south of England, in the little town of Hungerford, in the County of Berkshire, life was slow, pleasant, and some might say 'laid back', nevertheless, the doctors were skilled in their profession, (as they are today of course,) and most of them in that particular line of work did it out of a love for humanity and a dedication to their life's calling..

But, to return to our story, the doctor began to fill out the form as my mother watched, then, he looked in the box again to double check the lifeless little body within, he looked somewhat puzzled, picked up the limp form, slapped a little here and there, (you know where!!), shook it a little, then with a cry of protest I had arrived officially into the world. I realise now of course that I owe a lot to that dedicated doctor, but even more to the Power behind him that day, I could have been buried as a stillborn infant but The Lord planned otherwise.

Chapter Two

When Mom was stronger and finally brought me home, my sister Joan was really not too impressed, she would have preferred a new doll instead of a baby brother I am sure, she looked in the cradle where I smugly reposed and gave a non committal grunt, perhaps she could sense the future, a little brother can be a real drag for a little three year old girl. I will say here however that Joan saved me from serious injury or perhaps worse at one point in my early years, I was sitting in my high chair, now, to the reader who has not encountered one of these things, they tower about forty feet into the air, or so it seems to the overly energetic child who is strapped into one of these contraptions in order to restrain him or her from jumping out during a meal, also of course to raise the child to the level of the table so that the food thrown around during the mealtime struggle lands mainly on the table..

Mom had left the room for a moment and my little sister was watching over me, I decided I suppose that it would be fun to rock back and forth to see if it would be possible to escape, of course what happened next was predictable, over went the chair, but sister Joan with great presence of mind grabbed it and so prevented it from falling, thus saving me from hitting the floor, she screamed for Mom and sanity was restored.

Chapter Three

During the next few years we were forced to move from place to place, dad was a journeyman bricklayer and as a job ran out, or dad got into a scuffle with a fellow worker and quit, (as sometimes happened,) we would move on to an area in closer proximity to his new jobsite. Back then only the wealthy owned cars, we definitely did not fit into that category. Dad owned a bicycle and would have to ride to work in all weather, poor dad, his hands would bleed from handling bricks all day, his hands were hard and calloused from working outside and having to ride perhaps several miles home at the end of the day, in the pouring rain or snow depending upon the season of the year, as children we do not realise, and in many cases not appreciate what our parents go through to keep the home together.

We lived for a while in the village of Burghclere, it was here that I started school, no kindergarten mind you, but straight into the first grade of elementary school, fate dealt me a cruel blow at this point, as my birthday fell in early September somehow in order for me to fit into the school admission program I actually had to start at the tender age of five, life, apart from the school that I hated, was fun, we had a rural property with fields and woods nearby, there was a small creek running under a little wooden bridge close to our house, the area was part of the 'Ox drove', so named because many years previously oxen were driven along the narrow gravel road on their way to market, Mom was able to lay over this bridge and actually 'tickle' the large brown trout that swayed lazily in the current beneath and throw them up onto the bank of the stream, we had many a tasty meal as a result of this strange behaviour, but then, Mom was a survivor, as we would say nowadays..

We kept goats, rabbits and chickens, in addition Mom and Dad always worked a small garden, English people are noted for this, Dad grew all the vegetables we needed, we never had to buy milk, meat or eggs, I never tasted anything but goats milk for years, I should say in passing that if a person is careful in their selection of animals there is no need for any odour that many people associate with goats, furthermore I do not profess or claim to be a nutritionist but apparently cows milk is very difficult for the human body to assimilate, whereas goats milk is more compatible with our human system, my mother will attest to that, she gave it to us as an infant formula..

Joan and I would wander along the banks of this same stream, we would go to see the Rhododendrons that grew wild in great profusion along the edge of the woods, we had deer and foxes, we always knew when we had surprised a fox, the musk odour in the air was unmistakeable, the climate was ideal for two children who loved the great outdoors, Joan and I would run barefoot along the narrow little path that bordered the creek, as carefree as two little children could be, this brings us to another miracle, seemingly minor, but it could have had serious consequences--

One day Dad came along this path to tell us that it was suppertime, he had never previously had to do this as we were usually home on time, he saw us coming in the distance, he also saw the big Viper coiled up on the trail where we would have arrived moments later, running and laughing and not looking for such a creature, Dad killed it with a stick, we went to see it later, it was only about four feet long I suppose, but as thick as Dad's wrist, the Viper, or Adder is a member of the pit Viper family, England's only poisonous snake but I believe as deadly as the North American Rattlesnake, perhaps even more so, in addition to this there is no warning rattle and they have a personality on a par with a 'junkyard dog', the reader may gather from this that I do not like snakes, and you are correct.

We were far from any hospital, no transportation, no phone, do you think it mere co-incidence that Dad came along that very day to call us for supper,? he had never done this before, no, I personally believe that our Heavenly Father was on the path that day. I know that many people scoff at the idea of a 'Personal', or guiding Angel, or even a serious belief in the 'supernatural', but the circumstances that follow in this book, as my life unfolds, convinced me that He was not only on the pathway beside that little creek but on the pathway of life that we follow on a daily basis.

Chapter Four

During the next few years I pursued the normal life of a child, climbing trees, falling from trees and other objects, skinning knees and elbows, somehow poor Joan got most of the blame for my minor injuries, she was supposed to be looking after me so Mom had a tendency to blame her for the foolish things that I did the moment her back was turned. Joan dragged me to school, literally, she loved school as much as I hated it, she was almost always late because of me, my fault and I admit it, there were small ponds to explore, small streams to check out for any signs of life. In the fall there were great piles of vivid coloured leaves to jump into, kick around, or, better yet to throw at Joan until she threatened to tell Mom, in those days it was not considered a crime to spank one's own offspring and I collected my 'dues' from time to time, isn't it strange how I loved my Mom in spite of all the whacks on the rear that I collected, I see children today who's parents would not even dream of raising their voices to their children in case it would harm their relationship in some way, unfortunately they often have no respect for their parents in later life. The old 'Spare the rod and spoil the child' seems to make sense, now of course a line has to be drawn between discipline and abuse, and thereby hangs the problem. Poor Joan, to return to my long suffering sister she would wail 'Mother, why do I have to take HIM along?

I remember the time that I thought it would be a great joke to lock Joan out of the house, both she and Mom were away for a few hours so I fastened all the bottom windows, locked the doors, the last one, an upstairs window locked when it was closed, I then hid in some bushes to see the results and watch the fun, my long suffering sister returned and almost went ballistic, so to speak, I chuckled to myself from my vantage point, then horrors, Mom came home without warning, it took the neighbour's long ladder and much effort to get an upper window open, boy was I sore and sorry after that episode!! I believe upon reflection that I calmed down considerably in the practical joke department, at least as far as my immediate family were concerned..

Chapter Five

When I was seven years old England declared war upon Germany, life as we knew it changed, there had been rumours of war as the Nazis began their advance into Poland, as a child I did not give it too much thought, neither did I understand it, this can be a blessing at times, children, at least in my humble opinion should be allowed to enjoy life as a child, the cares and worries of adulthood come upon us all too quickly! I remember this young lady friend of Mom's who would call by and visit, and I remember her hair style for some reason, she had a big roll of hair crosswise on the front of her head as was probably the style in 1938-39, her name was Joy, She liked to read the papers and would often say, 'There's gonna be a war'

Dad called her 'Oh be joyful', in fun, it turned out that her favourite expression was prophetic however.

War was declared, as Joy had so often prophesied, and the young men in our sleepy little village of Boxford were called up in short order, blackout and rationing arrived but it was accepted as a necessity, and, as in World War One, nobody imagined in their wildest nightmares that it would last as long as it did. There was a little general store next door to us at number 80, Boxford, it adjoined our house, had the same picturesque thatched roof, the lady who operated the store had a young son who had enlisted in the Royal Air Force, or RAF, as it was generally called.

I will remember to the end of my days one of the worst moments in my young life as one morning she came running from the store screaming, 'He's dead, he's dead', as she waved a telegram over her head, she was crying and totally out of control, the telegram was from the war office to notify her that her young son had been shot down on a bombing mission over Germany, he failed to bail out it would seem, this scenario of course was played out in many families throughout the land, it only brings out the horror and complete stupidity of warfare, in England's case however, had she and her Allies chosen to do nothing the Axis hoards would possibly have taken over the entire world and I would not have had the freedom to write this book, Adolf Hitler had this dream of a 'Super Race' and a One thousand year reign', however God was, and is, in complete charge and it was not in the Master Plan.

We had a cartoon character in England at the time, Mr Chad, as he was called, he appeared everywhere, his long nose always hanging over a wall with a 'Wot no' caption below, usually 'Wot no butter?' or 'Wot no eggs? 'I never really did decide why he was called Mr Chad but humour of any kind was always welcome in those war years to boost the morale of the population. After dark the blackout was total, if one struck a match it would seem an air raid Warden would knock on the door and ask you very politely to be more careful, road signs were all removed to confuse the enemy should they land on our shores, I suspect they did more to befuddle the residents and even more so the US forces who set up their base camps at a later date in the area. Soon the German Luftwaffe were flying overhead on their way to targets in Newbury, and further on to London, we were about sixty miles from that great city that bore the brunt of the enemy's fury.

We were not too concerned about the possibility of a raid on our village but the planes flew over day and night, mostly during the night. We could distinguish between the incoming enemy bombers and the outgoing RAF aircraft by the sound of their engines, much like being able to tell the difference between a Chevrolet pickup truck and a Ford pickup, it has something to do with the beat of the engine I suppose, we would lay in bed and say 'That's one of ours, or," One of theirs!". We were all issued gasmasks as there was a danger of mustard gas being dropped from the air, the reader might assume that we lived in a state of constant fear, this however was not the case, we accepted our position, moral was high during those war years, we did whatever we could on the home front to support our troops overseas. We had a great 'waste not, want not' attitude, all the unwanted aluminum pots were carefully collected, donated by the womanfolk at home, that is between working in the factories and the Woman's land Army, a regular force of ladies of all ages who worked the land while the menfolk were absent.

I recall one night walking home in the dark across a pasture, a big open field, when I heard enemy aircraft overhead, I was not overly concerned, they would not waste munitions on little old Boxford, a sleepy village in Berkshire where I presently lived, then suddenly the whole field lit up around me, the aircraft had dropped a flare for some reason, this was probably done to survey the area below to check for possible targets, I felt like an actor on center stage, the grass, perhaps eight inches tall now must have towered above me as I flattened out in the very roots of the grass, the flare burned out after a few minutes and so did I, straight for home, upon reflection I got plenty of exercise during those war years.

Life had it's humorous moments of course, a person would tend to forget the war that was not a factor in everyday life, or so it seemed!

I was blissfully picking blackberries one day, in a spot known as the 'chalk pit', solid limestone cliffs surrounded a flattened out area where both blackberries and snakes prospered, there were the harmless grass snakes and the highly poisonous Viper, or Adder, as the locals called them. The home guard used the limestone cliffs as a backdrop for their target practice, we were not supposed to be in the area of course, even when there was no action taking place, it was while digging the spent bullets out of the limestone that I discovered the fossils from the past, there were perfect specimens embedded in the chalk, of course in my youth the significance of such a find was lost upon me, when we return to England one day I intend to re-visit this very interesting area.

Well --to return to the young lad picking berries into a sealer jar--I heard the enemy bombers flying over above the clouds but too high for me to actually see them, then I heard the RAF fighter planes coming up fast, the slow throb throb of the bombers engines picked up speed, what

I could not see of course was that in an attempt to evade the fighter planes the enemy aircraft simply opened their bomb bays, and just let it all go in one parcel, this caused the the planes to gain altitude in a hurry, but they were no match for the boys in the Spitfires, the load hit the ground about two miles away, at a place called the Chievely cross roads, and I swear to this day that the ground around me buckled. Roger Bannister was probably not the first man to run the four minute mile, I believe that I probably was, straight for home, I do not recall hearing the planes hit the ground as they were shot out of the sky, perhaps due to the air rushing past my ears as I departed in great haste, homeward bound.

As time progressed, the situation in the south of England worsened, sometimes children overhear things not meant for small ears, The German troops were firmly entrenched across the Channel in France, steady gunfire and the flashes of the heavy shore batteries lit up the night sky, the rumour was that an invasion was imminent, Winston Churchill told the British not to worry, he knew the danger, but preferred not to let the people know the grim reality, later records disclosed that Hitler had an invasion of the British Isles planned but changed his mind and diverted his attention to the invasion of Russia, a great mistake for the enemy, this was where they ultimately met their 'Waterloo'... I believe that God caused Hitler to change his mind at this point in history, England was in a very vulnerable position, to put it mildly---Dad was in the Home guard, a force of former first world war fighting men whose job it was to make a last stand on home soil should an invasion occur. Dad was naturally armed with the good old 303 Enfield rifle of that era, I heard him say to Mom 'When they attack, if we should lose, one shot is for you, one for each of the children, and the last one for me'! This was hardly music to the ears of a snoopy ten year old kid, but I never revealed my secret to anybody.

At about that time the V1s, or Buzz bombs, as they were generally called, began to fly over southern England, the principal of these nasties, being when they ran out of fuel they simply fell and exploded, they did little actual damage generally speaking unless they fell in a populated area, as some did of course, the main intent was to intimidate a war weary nation. I remember the great trenches that were excavated across the landscape, known as 'tank traps', they were designed with that very purpose in mind, they were thankfully never put to the test, of course they soon filled with water and both plant life and small fish appeared and flourished, I would spend many happy hours catching minnows in these man made ponds, Mom was no doubt worried as I would disappear in the mornings, net and 'jam jar' in hand, not to re-appear until suppertime, I did some really crazy things at this time in my life, I took a galvanized washtub down to the river Lambourne that flowed along the bottom of the allotment lands, (these were parcels of land that were rented out to the villagers to raise their own food,) I climbed aboard and proceeded to sail down the river, at this point I should mention that I could not swim a stroke!, my Angel was no doubt very busy in those far off but blissful days. Another pastime worth mentioning--In our school we would make rings for our fingers from heavy plastic, or perspex as it was known in those days, now you might ask where did we get our raw materials in those times of severe austerity?, well, from time to time planes would be shot down and crash out in the fields, the military would post a guard for a day or two until they could be hauled away, we would sneak out there in the dead of night and retrieve pieces of the shattered plastic windshields, we were taking a chance, we were risking a jumpy guard with a hair-trigger finger, it was not actually theft as the planes would go to the junkyard, but boys do strange things to enhance their image in school.

At this time in history my mother decided it was time to leave the south, the war was intensifying, the north of England was not affected by the 'buzz bombs', we owned a herd of goats and a couple of horses, we loaded them all in a boxcar and headed north on the GWR railway, we had to live in the 'Jockey box', the area designed to house the jockey when he transported his horses, a little crowded for the three of us, Dad did not come along, I found out later why, he had found what he considered 'greener pastures' and we were on our own. Even on this trip, life had it's tense moments, the authorities did not realize that we were aboard along with our precious animals, we were shunted off into a siding at Crewe station, along the Great Western line, all around us were tanker cars, full of fuel, we heard the air raid alarm in the nearby town, heard the enemy aircraft, also some anti-aircraft fire, but by the Grace of God they did not hit that siding--We did not realize at that point in our lives that He had His shield over us. Mom had a friend in Cumberland, in northern England, she was also a fellow goatkeeper, we combined our 'herds', and settled down to our new life.

Chapter Six

As time went on we disposed of our livestock due to a lack of suitable pasture land and rented and lived in an ancient house actually built on Hadrian's wall, this wall was constructed under orders of the Roman Emperor Hadrian during his occupation of England centuries before, it stretched from coast to coast across the northern part of the country, it had in it's heyday been over two chariots wide with forts at certain intervals, the area that our house occupied had been the site of one of these forts. Much of it now had sunk into the ground or been carried away during the centuries. As a young person I was not too interested in the ancient history surrounding me, the house was a huge stone edifice with massive stone slabs for flooring, great hand hammered iron hinges supported the thick and ancient wooden doors that creaked and groaned in protest as they were opened, huge hand hewed slates formed the roof, I had nightmares surrounding this house for years afterwards, Alfred Hitchcock could have written volumes, using our house as a model for ghost stories. I was also having a little difficulty with the language at this point, the children in the local school all spoke with the Northumberland, or 'Geordie' accent, it is different from the Berkshire accent, and to me at that stage in my life I might as well have been in a totally different country, I felt totally isolated, having always been something of a'loner', the other children called me a foreigner, and so it seemed to me at least, that I was, but as in all things we learn to adapt.

One thing that surprised me was the difference in climate, in the south of England, in the village of Boxford, only 300 miles or so away we lived in a thatched cottage that would have made Anne Hathaway proud, (alluded to earlier, at 80 cornerways), the house is still there but is known as '80 Boxford' at the present time, sometimes we would have a sprinkling of snow on the rooftops, the warm sun would soon turn the light white frosting into vapour that would rise up in a lazy swirl from the thatch, I loved Boxford, yes, and I still do, enough of my dreams of the south, now I had real cold weather to contend with. One of my school friends rode to school past our house and as I did not own a bicycle at that time in my life he offered to ride me on his handlebars in the mornings, he was a very wise lad, I made the perfect windshield, I would arrive at school, a half frozen wretch and stand by the huge barrel heater that one of the older boys would stoke with wood, coming home was easier, it was all uphill, a good stiff walk and in places alongside portions of the Roman wall that had been excavated for public display, one thing that amazed me was the way the huge stones had been hand cut to fit together so precisely, in our 'plastic world' we see no evidence of the painstaking work of yesteryear, mind you, having a Roman soldier with a big whip standing alongside might have inspired those poor slaves to do their very best!..

Chapter Seven

In time we moved to the village of Gilsland, a pretty little village on the edge of the moors, made famous by the playright Sir Walter Scott, I finally adapted to my new lifestyle, exploring the countryside, fishing in the river Irthing, a river that at times would be brown from the colouration of the peat bogs through which it flowed, through the moorlands further up stream, it was a grand fishing river and I made the most of it whenever possible. When not fishing or attending school I would be trapping moles for a local farmer, he paid me so much per head, (the heaps of soil they left in his hayfield raised havoc with the mower blade), checking out the new and different birdlife and wildlife in the area and generally having fun. In time I graduated from school and joyfully made my way home, papers in hand skipping and singing 'free at last', enroute I encountered my good wise friend, Stobbart Smith, now Stobbart worked for the village and could usually be found digging in some ditch, I liked him a lot, he was a type of mentor I suppose, he was also a very wise man, probably not in terms of education as one is so often judged today, but he was a type of 'Will Rogers' I suppose, he looked at me sorrowfully and said 'The best days of your life are now behind you! 'I could not believe that this man, who's advice I had always cherished, could come out with such an irrational statement, however my mothers favourite expression, 'You can't put an old head on young shoulders', certainly applied in this case.

I headed out in life with no particular plan in mind, a bold sense of adventure overshadowed any sense of direction, as a young teenager who obviously thought himself immortal I was no different from any other lad of that era, mind you the opportunites available today did not really exist back then, unless of course your parents were especially 'well heeled' as the expression goes.

My Mother worked hard to support us, and she did a fine job, all things considered, welfare did not exist then, and he who did not work did not eat, my first concern was to find a job, I attached myself to a local farmer, the same farmer who had employed me to rid his fields of moles, where I experienced all the delights of cleaning out the cowbarn, or 'byre,' to use the local terminology, milking, which could be a blessing on a cold winter morning, snuggled up against one's favourite cow, or making hay out there in the field until ten o'clock at night, and 'Don't you even think about going home early, not if you wanted your job lad! 'He had been a Major in the first world war and somehow he never forgot this previous position of ultimate authority. He kept a particularly ferocious bull in one of the stalls, it was safely enclosed in a steel stanchion, this held the huge miserable beast captive with a secure neckhold until my boss, with much greater bravery than I would ever exhibit, would lead him from his stall by virtue of a snap device on the end of a long pole, hooked into his big brass nose ring, I would make myself very scarce at these times, frankly I was scared of this great beast with his rolling eyes and constantly slobbering mouth, when I cleaned out his stall he would roll his eyes back at me, bellow and kick, I learned to avoid his flailing back legs and regarded him as the devil in the flesh.. a short time afterwards and many miles away I was informed that my former boss had been killed, gored by a bull, some how I really expected this to happen, I hope that they converted 'Diablo Toro' into dog food, I love all animals, this was one exception to the rule..

One day while checking the local paper I noticed an ad under 'help wanted', it was for a fourth gardener at the nearby mental hospital, as such facilities were known in those 'pre- politically correct' days, now I have always loved gardening, and to this day I still do, why not get paid for a more enjoyable line of work than dodging the old bull's back legs down on the farm?. I applied at the office, the superintendant looked at me sadly and said 'You are a little young for the job at 17 years of age, but you look like a big strong lad, you may start on Monday". This reference to my size and strength led me to believe that I would be expected to perform great gargantuan tasks of hard labour, as it turned out however this was not the case. One of the other senior gardeners took me to the bottom of a flight of stairs, unlocked the door with a large iron key, where he called out about seven or eight names, a few moments later in response to his call a number of fellows appeared in work garb, this procedure was repeated in several locations until we had a sizeable crew. We then proceeded to the garden area, a really huge acreage, I might add, where there were dozens and dozens of wheelbarrows. Each man took a wheelbarrow, I went to get one, but my fellow worker restrained me, "No' he said, "We are to instruct and watch, not to work'. The whole day was then spent moving leaf mold from a giant heap out into the garden area, at intervals my colleague would call, 'Ok lads, lets have a rest', everybody would then sit on their wheelbarrows until he told them to carry on. This was actually a good form of therapy, the patients were much happier out in the garden than moping about in the wards, we did not work them hard, and, all the vegetables used in the kitchens were grown on the premises. There was also a large farm in the area belonging to the institution where pigs were raised, also for consumption on the premises. This system could well be copied in today's world, we were not exploiting them, they were happy to be out with us, many of them could carry on a good conversation and we were encouraged to be a friend to the lads wherever possible. Now I realized where stature was an advantage, after I was given my own key and collected my own crew from the wards they would not regard me as a boy, sometimes the odd person would be a little stubborn, it helped to be a little taller than my 'charges'. Incidently, this particular episode in my life helped me when I applied for a position as prison guard, many years later and far away in another country..

The moorlands of northern England were windswept, wild and desolate and yet peaceful with perhaps the only creatures in sight a few sheep, the constant call of the Curlew, a bird who's haunting cry never really leaves one's memory, the stone walls that serve as boundary markers that run on forever to the skyline and beyond, the occasional harsh croak of a Raven, the Plover, or lapwing that would dive bomb precariously close to a person's head during nesting time, a sure indication that the nest, lined with grass and feathers and built in a slight hollow on the ground was very close, if this failed then the old 'broken wing trick' would be utilised, the poor bird would limp along the ground, dragging it's supposedly broken wing, crying piteously, but, if pursued, it would suddenly rise up, perfectly and miraculously healed, now that the animal or human were far enough away from the nest. These were my only companions as I walked alone, and yet I was never alone, as events later in this book will verify, it has been said to walk in a garden one is close to God, this could well be true but to wander over those vast reaches of moorland is to experience an inner peace that has no explanation at the time, as we grow older and hopefully wiser we can look back and recognise the Source of this inner peace.

The English woods were a different story however, the springtime can only be described as delightful, the bluebells, which are really wild hyacinths, would carpet the ground amid the hardwood trees, baby rabbits were hopping and skipping in the warm sunshine, primroses grew wild along the hedgerows, new life was everywhere, a huge pussy willow humming with bees, gathering pollen from the big golden tassels was a favourite spot of mine, where I would climb up into the branches and just simply sit and take in all the heady aromas of the wildflowers below. I could also watch the baby rabbits skipping with all the joy that only baby animals can experience. Songbirds were nesting and the woods were filled with their song, Chaffinch, Goldfinch, Bullfinch, Greenfinch, Robins, [a little different from the American Robin, which is really a Thrush], the one thing that I really miss most of all, even to this day would be the English woods.

I have no idea what Heaven will be like, it is written in the Bible that there will be things so beautiful as to be beyond the imagination of man, I hope that God will forgive me if I would like to see just a little of the joys of the English woods in springtime, when my wife and myself, sometime in the future, visit my previous homeland, very little time will be spent in the cities, much time will be spent enjoying the scents and sounds of the woodlands, wandering among the bluebells and listening to the birdsong. Canada is now my home, I am a Canadian citizen but have never relinquished my English status.. Canadian forests are so silent, Gordon Lightfoot puts it into true perspective with his song, "The tall dark forests are too silent to be real" in his 'Railroad Trilogy', the huge trees are so lacking in bird song, when I first stood in the woods in Canada I felt a dreadful foreboding, in fact I can only describe it as being scared,, the only time this would happen in England would be just before a thunderstorm, birdsong would be silent, it were as if all the creatures were waiting for that first peal of thunder..

Mom and I rented an upstairs suite in a huge house just outside the village limits of Gilsland, built of stone, as was the fashion in that area, with great stone gargoyles that held up the rain gutters overhead, there was certainly a wealth of stone in the north of England, I loved to play silly pranks, as all young people do, in fact, upon reflection, I have never really outgrown this trait. The narrow side roads in that area where we lived were banked up steeply on either side, with the inevitable stone wall topping the rise, large oak trees grew in the stone walls, I attached a length of chain to one branch than reached out well over the centre of the road, by holding on firmly I was able to swing right across to the other side, landing at the base of the opposite wall, no doubt inspired by the Tarzan comics, I would wait for a vehicle to approach, then swing right across the victims car or truck, only inches to spare between my hurtling body and his front bumper, of course the result was the shrieking of rubber on the road surface as the driver came to a violent stop to avoid this lunatic passing in front of his windshield, followed by loud curses, much fist shaking and threats from the red faced motorist as I made good my escape over the wall.

One day that I will always remember, I was making a trial run over the road, largely out of boredom as no vehicle had come my way for a while, then the unthinkable happened, being a little short of materials, (and obviously even shorter on brains,) I had wired two pieces of chain together with some old rusty wire I had salvaged from somewhere, it was here that I learned the truth in the expression', A chain is only as strong as its weakest link', the weak link namely the wire, broke, and I fell unceremoniously to the road surface below, landing in my crouched position my knees came up to my jaws and needless to say I did not eat anything until the swelling receded. That was the end of this particular prank, probably just as well, I am sure that in time I would have had a visit from the village 'Bobby' had I kept it up..

I never did tell Mom. things were embarrassing enough, I invented some wild tale I suppose to explain it away, at that time in my life I did not consider lying to cover one's mistakes a sin, I believe that 'white lie' was the expression used!. One strong point I would like to make in this part of the story. What if a vehicle had been right there instead of this being a practice run? I had a particularly nasty expression I would use, one that my wife had to cure me from using years later, it was 'The devil looks after his own', now I know that 'The Lord looks after HIS own', even when we don't realize it, or worse, don't even care,

He looks down through the years and of course knows what we will become, I think that's pretty neat to say the least. Mom bought some books for me to read by Richmal Crompton, they were the adventures of a boy entitled 'Just William' the adventures of this boy of course only existed in the mind of the author, Mom was not so sure that he was purely fictional, some of the crazy pranks that I 'pulled off' would closely parallel the adventures of William in the book.

Downstairs in the huge stone house previously described, lived a couple of newlyweds, Gus and Anne Atkins, a wonderful couple, I often wonder where they are now, they always invited me for Sunday dinner, she was a great cook and I loved to eat, what boy of seventeen doesn't, Gus felt sorry that I had no Dad and basically took me under his wing, he built a toboggan out of wood, with iron runners, painted bright red, he gave it to me one winters day and I dragged my little treasure for many miles. He drove a delivery truck for a local company and would sometimes take me on his rounds, I would help with the loading and unloading, even though I suspect this was not company policy.

One day I was leaning on the door, daydreaming of course, when the door of the truck suddenly flew open, I took a headlong dive on to the road at full highway speed,

I curled in a ball and rolled alongside, I recall seeing the truck in little flash images as I rolled, Gus stopped as soon as he was able to, very shaken up of course, it was a miracle that I did not go under the wheels, all I suffered was a skinned hand, needless to say I was now very much awake, at the time I thought how lucky I was, now I know that luck, whatever that might be, had nothing to do with it. Gus by the way would never take me out again after this incident, I could hardly blame him for this.

Thankfully the second world war came to a close, the newspapers were full of photographs taken by the liberating forces, of the concentration camps, of the poor wretches, skin and bone, barely alive, I remember these pictures vividly, let nobody even suggest that it did not happen, or that it was a cooked up hoax, it was the ultimate satanic horror, some of the Allied forces who came upon the mass graves and gas chambers were even affected mentally by this experience, but the German people as a whole did not realise what was taking place, they had been persuaded, and as the saying goes 'brain washed', by their news media that the Jews were the cause of all their problems, this is a lie straight from hell, we can not hold this against them, somebody was once asked if he could prove the existence of God, he answered "The Jew"--No other race of people could have possibly survived the persecution that these people, who are truly 'God's chosen', have endured throughout the centuries. Soon re-patriation of the 'ex-enemy' prisoners back to their own countries, took place. We had befriended an ex prisoner of war who worked on the same farm as I, Robert was a tall lean fellow with a good command of the English language, he was soon to return home to Germany but lacked a decent suit of clothes, my favourite uncle had passed on previously and in his effects, left to Mom, was a complete and beautiful suit, the suit fitted Robert perfectly, not by chance or co-incidence, all things happen for good, Mom gave the suit and her blessing to an overjoyed Robert, who promised one day to send for us for a holiday in Germany for the moment this was all forgotten..

Chapter Eight

Now we find a young man, namely myself, longing for adventure. Mom was always game for anything, we both felt somewhat trapped in life and soon we were looking at maps, at that time it seemed to be either Canada or Australia in our sights. The Australian Govt were looking for crocodile hunters, I was a crack shot and proud of it, this seemed to be a great idea, the persons selected were to be accompanied by at least two Aboriginals, they were to be both guides and skinners, I certainly gave this idea lots of thought although I think my mother was not as keen on the plan as I was at the time. I was now nineteen years of age, a person who loved to hunt and fish, no girlfriends to hold me back, hunting and fishing took care of that, when most young men of my age were dreaming of some particular girl I was roaming the moorlands with a twelve gauge shotgun... At this point God intervened in my plans, He knew exactly where we were to go..

Then suddenly, out of the blue so to speak came a letter from Robert, remember Robert from some years back? The letter was from Mud River, Prince George, British Columbia Canada, he was working on a farm in the area, but was shortly moving to an orchard in Summerland, in the South Okanagan Valley, called 'Paradise Ranch' and described the countryside, the abundance of wildlife, the hunting, the fishing, it all sounded just wonderful, he had decided to live in Canada and begged us to come and experience the joys and freedom of his newly discovered land, so, after giving this some consideration we sold the little wooden house that we owned, got all our papers in order, passports, tickets etc, sold everything that would not fit into five suitcases and took the train from Carlisle in Cumberland to Southampton down in the southern part of England. As we travelled on via the Great Western Railway the trees were in leaf and the crops were so far advanced compared to the north, that we had a feeling of deep sorrow to be leaving England, in fact I believe that had we never left our beloved Berkshire we would possibly be there to this day, but, even as I say this, I know that God had a plan for my life that definitely involved coming to Canada. We boarded the MV. Georgic at Southampton and set sail, for Halifax Nova Scotia.

On the first leg on our journey, we felt like Columbus, heading for the new world, except we knew where we were going with a little more security than that brave fellow. It was a bittersweet moment as the tiny tugs down in the English Channel below pushed our ship out to the point where the big diesel engines could safely take over, the crowds on shore waving goodbye to their loved ones gradually receding into the distance, we had no farewell party to see us off, it was mom and I, heading out to a new life, my sister Joan had decided to stay in England, she thought at the time we were, as the saying goes 'A few bricks short of a load', she was convinced I believe, that our new land was inhabited by savages, and that we would surely meet our end in our new found Country, in fact she was so worried for Mom's safety that she followed us out two years later.

Our first stop was in Cork Harbour, in Ireland, where we loaded on a few more travelers, then on, across the mighty Atlantic Ocean, it was a very rough passage with very high seas once we reached mid ocean, we had to change course and sail further north in order to avoid a pretty serious weather pattern Here again upon reflection at a later date, my Saviour, who at that date I still did not know, or acknowledge, had His hand upon me..

I loved to sit out on the deck, on a small seat, bolted down, and up against one of the hatchways and stare out to sea, on this particular day the seas were very rough, I assumed that everybody else must be sick and below decks, I wondered why I was the only person in sight!, I was shortly to find out the reason for this!

Most of the passengers were below deck as a warning had gone out to stay off the deck, I had not heard this warning due to a very noisy group who wandered around the deck yelling, drinking and playing a very loud musical instrument, the messages would come out over the intercom in three languages, first "Attention please", then the message in English, next "Achtung achtung" and the message in German, during all this it was impossible to decipher due to the noise from these fellows, and of course the roaring of the waves, then it would be delivered in French, the silence was instant, of course this was no help to me as I did not speak the language. I should have realised that when the noisy fellows disappeared that something was afoot. It was quite an odd sensation as our ship ploughed along, one moment there was no water in sight as we crested a wave, the next it seemed as though we were plunging down never to return, with huge seas towering above our relatively tiny ship, the 28.000 ton Georgic, then suddenly a great roar behind me as a huge wave came over the deck and tried to tear me loose, needless to say I had such a stranglehold on that little bench, for a few moments I could see nothing but the water pouring down all around and over me, at that point I knew why the bench was so well attached, a great flood of water tore across the deck and out under the guardrail, had I been swept out to sea at that point, with nobody else in sight I would certainly not have survived. I then took my soaking wet self back below deck, with more than just a sigh of relief. It has been my experience in life that He is always there, sometimes we have no time to call for help but He knows exactly when we need Him, as later events in this book will reveal.

I should say at this point, we were never seasick, for a while Mom and I were almost alone at our table, we had a Swedish waiter, who would ask 'Soup sair? with his amusing accent at the commencement of a meal, I loved to eat, and the food supplied by the Cunard Line was great, also paid for previously of course which spurred me on even more! Many of my "shipmates' spent most of the trip lying on their bunks groaning, of course down below deck one was even more aware of the ships motion, it was March, 1952, probably not the best time of year for an ocean cruise.. The rest of the trip went without further incident, due in part to my newly kindled attention to the messages on the PA system and also the fact that the weather and the high seas settled down somewhat.

so different from my homeland where the houses are generally in sombre tones of either brick red or stone gray, the engine pulling us along was to me straight out of a western movie, we had the good fortune to travel on one of the old steamers, before the railroad converted to diesel, The Good Lord must have known how much I wanted to travel behind a steam locomotive, the engineer blew the whistle as we left Halifax and there it was, the genuine sound of the old west, so far removed from the shrill whistle of our locomotives back in England. The smoke poured back alongside the carriages, and into any window carelessly left open, it would have been quite difficult to close our window for the simple reason that a young fellow was hanging out of the thing, grinning like a Cheshire cat and loving it. I was John Wayne, The Sundance Kid, and Gary Cooper, all rolled into one!..

We traveled on, mainly through the more northerly parts of the provinces, not much to see except the huge expanse of my new land that simply boggled the mind, night and day we traveled west, the "clack clack" of the joints in the steel rails becomes so imbedded in a persons conscience that I could still bring it to mind years later. The snow covered forests of northern Ontario and Quebec, small lakes and rivers everywhere, we stopped and changed trains in Quebec city, the brightly painted horse drawn carriages were a sight to behold, on across the wide prairies, much of the travelling at night, into the mountains of BC, through Jasper, huge towering mountains that made our Pennines, considered 'mountains' in England mere 'molehills' in comparison, Finally here we were, in Prince George, British Columbia. We walked into a restaurant for a coffee, I believe that it was called "the Dragon Cafe", the juke box was playing, Hank Williams was beating out "Honkytonk blues" loggers were sitting with their caulked boots up on the counter, probably daring anybody to ask them to take them down. Quite a contrast to the white table cloths on the little round tables in the cafe's back home, I was really impressed, we had arrived, I did a considerable amount of reading, back in England, mostly westerns, this was my idea of Dodge City, the streets in Prince George were mostly gravel in 1952.. Mom was also impressed, but not entirely in the same way, she was still the 'English lady', not quite 'Miss Kitty' from 'Gunsmoke' at that point in our lives..

We had arranged to be picked up by a Govt agent from the Dept of Agriculture, immigrants were required to state their intended occupation in order to be accepted in Canada, of course having worked on a farm all this went quite smoothly, a farmer out in Red Rock, near Prince George said "yes" he could use a couple of workers, so the Agent took us out to his farm. I found myself out in the middle of a field of stumps on the following day, axe in hand, lunch in a brown bag, I was supposed to cut the stumps out and pile them, not the most glamorous job in the world but I did not mind, I would tell myself that we all must start somewhere. My employer was not too demanding, "just keep chopping and piling" was all that he asked..

One evening, after two weeks of chopping and piling I was a little tired and a little cranky also, Mom had made some rice pudding using the water from the barrel outside the door of our cabin, the farmer kept it filled, it was our only source of water, the rice pudding she had made was terrible, it tasted like motor oil, it did not take long to trace the cause to the evil looking oil slick on the water surface on the barrel outside, I went up to the farmhouse to ask the reason for this!!.. "Oh yes," my worthy employer drawled; "I guess I used that barrel for sheep dip, I reckon I didn't clean it up too well". The reader may gather from this attitude that he really didn't really care, apparently this man would try to secure new 'off the boat' immigrants, work them until they quit, and then apply for new hired help, this was probably the first time that he had encountered a wild Englishman having a really bad day..

I am not going to disclose at this point what was said, the family were sitting at supper, I really was a wild man, ready to take on the world if need be, I had a few well chosen words to say. At this time in my life I did not know The Lord, and I was not really about to forgive this man for a mistake or just plain carelessness that could have made Mom and I really sick. I will only say that he wrote out a paycheck on the spot, his hand shaking like a leaf as he wrote. As I look back on these incidents in life I am not at all proud of them, there is word in the Bible that states 'A soft word turneth away wrath', I have put this to the test in the intervening years and found it to be so true!. I would also like to add at this point in the story that we are required to forgive those who harm or despise us--Christ forgave those who did far more harm to Him than a simple act of carelessness on this farmers part, in fact it is clearly stated in the Bible that our personal forgiveness is directly linked to our foregiveness of others, not just, 'Well ok, I forgive him, (or her)', but a really heart felt 'inward' feeling that only comes with practice, clearly I was not quite ready for this experience.

The next morning found us on the roadside, hoping for a friendly motorist to pass by, everything we owned repacked into five suitcases, after a short while along came a Carsons freight truck, a very friendly driver picked us up and took the two hoboes, Mom and I, back to Prince George. We checked into the Keller House, the only actual hotel in town, on the recommendation of the truck driver, giving Mr Keller the paycheck I had received the previous day, now we were precariously short of money, how was I to know that The Lord of All was guiding us and looking down at us even then?.. I had a really bad experience at this point in my life, during the night I developed a severe pain in my lungs, I sat up in bed, hardly able to breath, I was unable to call for help, not even to get out of bed, there was the usual hum of activity from the hotel below, I was quite scared, I even wondered if I was going to die there--However, in time the pain receded and now, looking back, I believe that the enemy tried to destroy me that night, remember that satan can only do what God permits him to do, if this were not so then all believers would be wiped out in short order..

The next day found me in the Prince George Unemployment office, things ran on a laid back, but perhaps more efficient system than the present day, one simply showed up, sat down and waited to be picked up by a prospective employer, my heart sank into my boots, a huge line up of men stretched from wall to wall, some of them big tough men, certainly bigger and tougher looking than I, times were rough and work was scarce in Prince George in 1952, men stood along the wooden sidewalks in that town with their hands out asking for a dime or a quarter, I began to wonder if I should have stayed with the farmer at Red Rock, whose gray ashen face I could still remember as he wrote out that paycheck, believing as I stood there that I probably intended to kill him. I was a wild man back in those days, many of my words and actions I regret, I am so thankful now that I know all that is forgiven by the acceptance of Jesus as my Lord and Saviour.

Back to the young man in the line up. A big fellow in a gray stetson hat walked in, a big fat cigar in his mouth, he looked slowly back and forth along the lineup, stopped, pointed at me and said "Are you looking for work, young fellow? "Wow! was I!!, I jumped up and almost beat him to the door, he was no doubt somewhat taken aback by my wild enthusiasm, he told me it was only stoking gravel, with the good old hand shovel into a cement mixer, I told him in return that it was fine, I needed the job, I could feel that he really liked me and I worked hard for him, it turned out that he was Mr Garvin Dezel, Mayor of Prince George in 1952 and owner of Dezel Construction.. A fine man I might add.

Chapter Ten

I soon began to realize that living in a hotel and eating in a restaurant ate up all of my wages, Mom had found a job at the Hospital, fortunately she had been a nurse in England so her experience helped, they would not accept her based on her nursing experience in England, so she took on the job of 'nurses aid'. One day I was out working in the rain, repairing a few potholes in the gravel street, which was normal in PG at that time, Dezel Construction took care of this also, it was part of their contract with the city, a man walked up and remarked "You don't look too happy my friend." Well I explained that it was not so much the job I was doing at the moment that was the problem, it was the lack of a future goal in life, of course he asked what else I could do, I told him that if I could find a big farm or ranch then Mom and I would be able work there and get out of the rut I was in, I certainly had enough experience with livestock back in England to qualify.. He said that he had friends down in Kersley, some miles to the south, apparently their ranch hand had just quit, notice the 'co-incidence?, more on this topic later. He took out a pen and paper and wrote down "Yorston brothers, Australian ranch" and a phone number, the call was made, Jack Yorston said "Come on down, we need some help"

The artist always depicts an Angel as a being with wings, glowing white, I suppose if that is the only way we could accept an Angel in our human minds then God would graciously present them in this fashion, however I personally believe that they can appear in human form, also of course God will direct a person to speak to a complete stranger to help him or her, why did that man approach me on the street in Prince George? In hindsight of course and looking back, I believe that it was not just 'pure luck'. Mom and I boarded the Greyhound bus with our well worn suitcases and made our way to the ranch, our home for the next two years, we moved into a a sturdy log house that had been a stage depot for the Cariboo stage run from Barkerville in a much earlier time in history, it was a warm and inviting old house, a big woodstove was the source of both cooking and heat, it was a source of wonder to Mom with it's huge oven and polished nickel trim, but it was home and we were very grateful.... The name Australian Ranch came from two Australian immigrants who, pushing a one wheeled cart, travelled the entire distance from Vancouver, BC, a distance of perhaps 350 miles on foot, following game trails through the bush until they found this beautiful spot close to the mighty Fraser River, they cleared the land, all by hand of course, with axe and crosscut saw, and it became known as "The Australian's Ranch". The PGE railroad had a siding and a loading dock for cattle nearby, this was no longer in use for that purpose but it is still known as 'Australian Siding...

To return to the two English immigrants in our story, we lived and worked on the ranch and loved it, we could not have worked for finer folk than the Yorstons, the two brothers Jack and Don ran the operation, it was mostly mechanized, as most ranches are in order to operate efficiently, we had a good sized herd of Hereford cattle however, I believe on average around 350 to 400 head--and one milk cow, thankfully Mom took over the morning and night chore of milking this beast, I had all the experience that I needed milking cows, the worst part is the wretched things have to be milked morning and night, day in, day out. I found other things of interest to do in the evenings. In the early fall or late summer the salmon would run up the Fraser to their spawning grounds far up river, somebody had constructed a plank walkway reaching out a few feet from the rivers edge, by packing branches and brush into the short upright posts supporting the structure it made a barrier to the huge sockeye salmon as they followed the easier route along the edge of this big swiftly flowing body of water, they were then forced to swim around the tip of this obstruction, I would stand on the end of the plank and keep up a steady pace with the big dip net, every few dips a huge struggling fish would be my reward, needless to say this practice was frowned on by the Dept of Fisheries, only native Indians were allowed to do this, this was soon rectified by rubbing charcoal from the wood fire upon any exposed skin, an old black stetson hat to top it off and I made a reasonably acceptable native, at least to the eyes of any fishery boats who might pass by. Along the rivers edge were large stands of Cottonwood trees, a type of Poplar, in the fall the leaves would turn a brilliant yellow and carpet the ground, they had a very pleasant fragrance, a sweet 'woodsy' smell, now whenever I pass by this species of deciduous tree in my travels in life, my mind goes back to those happy days on the ranch..

Mom canned salmon by the sackful, literally, we grew corn in the little garden and prospered. One rather amusing incident I will recount,. One of the other ranch hands lived on the premises, Albert was a Dutchman, a good mechanic, and a good worker, we got along very well exchanging stories of our previous experiences in life. Albert and his wife had a daughter, Ruth, she was a pretty little thing, very young at the time, about sixteen I believe. Ruth seemed to have a bit of a crush on me, but I was still in that "Roy Rogers" stage, not really much time for girls, one day we were standing by the little creek that ran by the ranch when I decided it would be fun to pretend to drop Ruth in the creek, I picked her up and started into the water intending just to scare her a little when her dog "Sparky" rushed up behind and bit the calf of my leg quite viciously, now I really did drop her in the creek as a result of the great pain in my leg, it was not too funny at the time I suppose but looking back I can see more humour in the incident, he was a good dog looking after his owner, from that day forward I re-named him "Sharky". Poor Ruth, I should have treated her a little better, she was lonely with no friends close by, I often wonder what became of her, if she reads my book she will remember the 'wild man who worked on the ranch'..

Chapter Eleven

Now of course I needed a vehicle, I purchased an Austin panel truck from one of the ranch hands, not a bad little machine, although Jack looked at it with a very sober face and said "You could have got a better car than that!", he was probably right, but I had no Dad to advise me, it had all the power of two sick sled dogs by todays standards, but now I was free, free to travel to Quesnel, our nearest town, and beyond. I soon spent more time fishing, exploring the lakes and rivers in the area, sometimes travelling through the native reserve to a lake called 'fish lake', there must be millions of lakes with this dubious title throughout our fair land, but this one really lived up to it's name, huge fish, if a little reluctant to bite, cruised it's murky depths, the little Austin had one advantage, I did not have to follow the huge 'bottomless' ruts left by the 4x4s, having a narrower gauge I could straddle one of the ruts and get about quite handsomely!. There was an old tumble down barn near the lake, remains of an earlier homestead, piles of hay from bygone years, smelly and dusty but a perfect place to sleep overnight so that I could be out on the lake at daybreak. I could hear packrats scuffling about during the night and occasionally one would hop over my ex-army sleeping bag, no doubt wondering who this large creature could be, but I did not bother them and they did me no harm...

As time passed I grew tired of the ranch life and explored other avenues in my new found land, soon the nearby sawmills beckoned, with their higher pay and of course harder work. Mom re-married a local man and went to live with him in his cabin, I found room and board with a nearby family. The Germaines were an honest hard working pioneer family, Jack was a long lean ex cowboy, tough as nails, didn't talk very much, he apparently had personally known some of the outlaw characters depicted in history books, although I must hasten to add he did not fit into their lifestyle.

Dorothy, his wife, was a rare gem, she was my Mothers best friend, in one of the darker chapters of our life in Canada when the strange and apparently demented man that she married decided to beat Mother up while I was safely far away in Vancouver, cowards act that way you know, whether school yard bullies or home place bullies, they will pick a time when their victim is either weak or alone, satan works in this fashion, Dorothy and the boys looked after Mom, I do not really want to go into details except to say that any man who beats a woman, especially a kind caring woman that my mother was, will one day face the ultimate judge, even if they escape retribution on this earth, as I mentioned earlier I had to deal with a case of forgiveness that took several years to materialize, at this point in my life I had not learned this very important principal-- enough said!.

Peter, one of Dorothy's three sons always liked to badger me over my accent, and some of the expressions I used, it was not long before I had to make adjustments to my vocabulary. The expression used to wake a person up the following morning in the English terminology was, 'I'll knock you up in the morning", the reader can easily see that such innocent expressions were not really going to fly in my new Country.

Two years or so after leaving the ranch, in the month of July, we had a particularly heavy and unusual period of rain to co-incide with a fast snow melt. A large tree came down the Australian creek and firmly wedged itself in the culvert under the road above the Australian Ranch, the road at this point was high above the ranch by virtue of a very deep road fill to bridge the small canyon 'that the creek, normally the quiet pleasant little stream flowing under the road, in which Kenny Yorston and myself fished in summer, was now a roaring brown torrent.

I went down with other local spectators to watch the inevitable horror, the creek backed up, way, way back to an old PGE railroad trestle far up the gorge, the water rose up to the level of the blacktop highway, a great lake glowering down upon the ranch below, somebody tried to get permission from the Govt Highway Dept to make a cut across the blacktop road, this would have allowed the water to cut the road away gradually from the top down, this would have averted the following disaster, it would seem that nobody in any Govt position can make a decision without first having a committee meeting, in short, it was refused Then the road and the man made dam buckled, a great wave of muddy water swept down upon the ranch, I watched our beloved log house with it's irreplaceable history, that had once been our home for awhile, the historic old stage stop from years ago ruined in moments, the big log barn, picked up like a doll house and smashed to pieces as the relentless brown flood carried it, together with mature cottonwood trees, further down stream, many pigs were lost that terrible day, to be carried down to the mighty Fraser river along with some of our fondest memories of the Australian.. Most of the main buildings survived, being on higher ground. Some of the old timers who watched, just wept silently..

I had some good friends in the nearby town of Quesnel, a couple of the R.C.M.P officers in the Quesnel detachment became friends. I will relate the following amusing incidents to show that life has it's funnier side. I had traded in my Austin van for a new 1955 Dodge car, while driving slowly through town one of the officers I recognised shouted very urgently from the side walk' Bill, stop,!, he leaped into the car, pointed ahead to a vehicle and asked me to 'follow that car', Wow!, now this was excitement, he instructed me not to get too close as he did not want the driver to recognise him. We continued along until we approached the traffic light at the end of the one lane bridge over into West Quesnel, at that moment a motorist tried to beat the light by rushing past us, changing his mind at the last second and stopping right in front of our car, now the light was red, the traffic coming toward us blocking our way, my Mountie friend in the passenger seat saying some very nasty things about the driver who had blocked us.

Well I wanted to know the story concerning the suspect in the car who had now vanished into the distance. It turned out that he thought it was his girlfriend in the vehicle we were pursuing, he wanted to get a closer look at the driver without being seen, so much for that adventure..

On another occasion I decided to go hunting during a particularly heavy snowfall, I had a heavy 'mummy' style sleeping bag, so I planned to sleep in the vehicle overnight, took along a few supplies including some cans of beans, the bachelors standby.. The temperature plunged to zero that night, by this I mean zero farenheit, I had missed a perfectly good shot at a deer that day so I snuggled down and waited for morning. At the first signs of dawn I lit a fire, set my can of beans on the fire and stood warming my back, suddenly a loud bang, beans all over the area including the back of my parka, I had forgotten in my haste to punch a hole in the can, at that point I packed it up and headed for home. I was a more successful fisherman than a deer hunter, perhaps because the former sport is pursued under more 'benign' conditions as far as temperature is concerned.

Chapter Twelve

The term "Break up" usually means in marriage or a business, in the Cariboo it means the time when all the roads, including the paved ones in the area become a hopeless mess of mudholes, potholes, swampholes and you name it!, this is caused by the long freeze up of winter finally loosening its hold upon the land, the mills would all shut down for several weeks, lumber could not be hauled, the side roads were officially closed to traffic. Now was the time to explore, I loaded my trusty vehicle and set out to see the Fraser Valley. The boys with whom I worked on the planer mill all spoke wistfully of Chilliwack, from their description it must have been close to Heaven, they were mostly single lads, I suspect that the girls in the area had a lot to do with their dreamy recollections of this potential Paradise.

I could hardly believe my eyes as I drove into Chilliwack, a small town on the lower Fraser river, behind me mud and melting snow, around me now, cherry trees in bloom, blue sky, birds singing, it was another world, and soon to be my world, it took only days to return to the Cariboo, pay off my bills, gather all that I possessed and return to my newly discovered Heaven. No more piling half frozen lumber, no more cutting water holes for the cattle in the creek in temperatures of minus forty farenheit, I had arrived. I scanned the local paper and found room and board with a family in town, next to find a job. I should add at this point in the story that even though there was not an abundance of work, especially in the Fraser Valley at that time of year I always walked right into a job as though I were expected, I was, I did not realize at the time Who was guiding me along the road..

The natural gas pipeline project had just started in the area, I hired on as a truck swamper and started work the next day, all the time I thought how lucky I was to sail through life always finding a job waiting, luck had nothing to do with it! now in my later years I realise that The Lord had His hand upon me even though I still did not know Him personally, I read somewhere that the word "luck" was derived from lucifer, I don't know if this is so but luck is not a word that I use any more. Later in this book I will show how He intervened dramatically in my life. We had a short shut down period for some reason, so I thought it a great time to rest from the seven day weeks that we were working at the time and explore.

The following account took place earlier in the story while I still owned the little Austin van, at the time I did not really consider it anything but that old 'luck thing' I loved to travel, to drive, to explore every avenue of my new country. While far from home and taking a long drive in the pouring rain one night I was so tired that it was impossible to drive further, it was an uninhabited stretch of road in the Sicamous area of BC, I suddenly saw what appeared to be a side road branching off to my right, it was shining in the headlights of the van and my next move was foolish to say the least, normally one would back up, check for obstacles, then drive in, I just backed up and cut my wheels hard, the next moment the little van was hanging over a bank, the side road, it turned out was a previous road, down at a lower level, a much lower level, Never drive when tired, lesson one. I left the vehicle in gear, opened the door and hung out on the door frame, this was the only way to stop the vehicle from rolling down the bank, the engine stalled in the process of course, there I was, wide awake by now, incidentally only my body weight stopping my uninsured little Austin from rolling over, one did not have to carry insurance back then! but what now??

I had not seen another motorist for hours, then, away in the distance, headlights appeared, in my minds eye I can still see that wonderful black Chevy car pull up beside me, out climbed the driver, a well dressed young man, all he said was, "My, you do have trouble, don't you?" he attached a rope to the his car and to my front frame, I could not move or the Austin would have rolled over, up we came, gently as a cork from a bottle, he jumped out, removed the rope, said "Goodnight and be careful" and as I was stuttering some heartfelt thanks, drove off into the night, now here again as I alluded to earlier, some might say how "lucky" that he came along, but now as I look back, was he a mortal, or an Angel? he didn't engage in the usual banter that one might expect, such as "where are you going or what are you doing? 'he just seemed to recognize the problem, acted and left.. this is all in hindsight of course, it is written in Hebrews 13-2, do not neglect to show hospitality to strangers, for by this some have entertained Angels without realizing it, so, from this we may gather that Angels can appear as men, yes, I really believe this to be so, but at this stage in my life The Lord was still the big Man with the stick, in my mind at least, waiting for me to mess up, and as the reader can gather, I was really good at "messing up"..

Chapter Thirteen

I returned home to Chilliwack, happily unscathed, and in one piece, continuing with my job on the pipeline.. At this time a small house came on the market in the rural area, I purchased the little house for the sum of four thousand dollars, a paltry sum by todays standards, but quite a pocketful back then, especially to a young fellow who did not even have a bank account, I had this amazing talent of being able to spend my wages at the same rate as I received them, I approached the local branch of the Royal Bank in Chilliwack for a loan and finances and to my amazement they accepted me and at last I had my own house.

Now I sent for mom, I was a miserable cook, (still am), and she came to live at the house, she loved the little house and fixed it up in the way only women can. The pipeline moved on, and so did I, into many different jobs, I worked as a driver on a freight truck, hauling freight from Kamloops to Vancouver, down through the Fraser canyon, for a company known as A and E transport, I enjoyed the work, always loved to drive, but in time the company, which ran on the proverbial shoestring, went bankrupt, so I moved on.

I worked as a prison guard for Oakalla Prison, in charge of inmates at the Forestry camps located up the Chilliwack river, I got along quite well with most of the unfortunates on my gang, they cleared brush, planted trees, and did many jobs for the forestry, even hand weeding small conifers that were slated for replanting, the men liked the work, no pressure was applied to them, they would tell me that it made the time go faster before their eventual release,

I had to stand, walk, be alert and constantly count heads, it was really quite a stressful job, usually if one of the prisoners decided to leave us prematurely it would be during the night, then the bed would be padded and one of our reluctant "guests" would be gone, one of the duties we had to perform was to make our rounds on the night shift and count the sleeping heads on the pillows, if one of the men escaped from our minimum security camps their punishment would be to serve out the rest of their time in Oakalla, back in the city, none wanted that so we had little trouble in that respect. We were encouraged to communicate with the inmates, as part of the rehabilitation program in force at that time, it was difficult to listen to some of the stories told without becoming emotionally involved, some of the tales were not true, several were totally unjust, some were, "I did it so what?

"One of the strange codes of honour, if you could call it that, involved the treatment of women and children on "the outside", if we admitted a new inmate who'se record showed rape, especially to a child, he was given a title, by the other inmates, not to be printed here, and he had to be closely watched, he would develop black eyes, bruises, cuts etc, and when asked how this happened he would look around and mutter 'I fell down', or some other excuse,.. How I wished now as I look back through the years that I had been a believer in those days, I am quite sure that I could have helped some of those unfortunates, there is a little streak of decency, if you want to call it that, in the vilest of men, witness for example.. Nicky Cruz.. his book, 'The Cross and the Switchblade', really points this out..

One example still sticks in my memory, we had a particularly troublesome fellow, of course I will not mention his name, the other guards had problems with him on their gangs, so,' Why not give him to Richens, see what he can do with him, well the very first day we were cutting up fallen trees for the Forest Service, to clear the woods of debris, this man would brag to the others that he "Would get him a guard before leaving, that the guards were yellow" and so on, this always so that I could just hear it, after our "brew up" time around the fire I sent him to do some work by himself, now bear in mind that this was minimum security, we were not armed. I then walked over to him and I said, "Very well, I have heard your story, as you intended, you are now on your own, now you may get your guard, here I am, this is your chance!..

He raised his axe above his head, I said "go ahead, but make sure that you don't miss, because if you do, then I will kill you" I said earlier that I was a wild man in those days, I put stock in my own speed and strength, how foolish, today I would have handled it differently, he held the axe over his head to see if I would back up, I did not so he laid his axe down then began to cry, he said it was nothing personal, the silence was deafening as the other inmates on my gang all watched from the distance, actually the guards are 'on trial' by the inmates, they judge a man by the way he handles sticky situations, I told him to go back to work and walked away, I was supposed to bring the whole gang in and put him in solitary according to rule, I don't always work to rule, he was a big man, obviously a proud man, an Italian, I decided that he was humiliated enough, nothing more was said and I did not make out the required report that would most certainly have sent him back to Oakalla.

After this he was a model on the gang, working happily, he would walk along beside me as my gang walked out to the bush, he would tell me about his girl friends on the outside, and in another time, another place, I am sure that he would have been a friend, oddly enough the other men seemed to respect me more from that day on, there are so many unfortunates out there, had I only been a believer in those days I would have realised that so many of the problems are spiritual, some people just need a listener, it could be a ministry in itself, if anybody feels the calling to be a prison Chaplain then I believe it would be one of the most worthwhile occupations possible for a person to have..

As a footnote, I read in the Vancouver paper a few years later of a man by the same name, (and he had a very unusual name), found stabbed to death in a Vancouver back alley, such is the way many meet their end, had I only known The Lord back then perhaps I could have helped this man, he needed a friend, I have an admiration for prison Chaplains, in many cases they are a blessing to a man such as this.

I owned a big heavy Chev pickup at the time, it was the perfect vehicle to drive back and forth to work at the prison camp when we were not using the guard service power wagon. We had to keep the private vehicles outside the gate and locked of course for obvious reasons, nevertheless the inmates knew who owned them. One day after having traded in 'Old Betsy', about one year earlier I saw my good old truck parked in town, I struck up a conversation with her new owner, he was pleased with the truck, however I then noticed the bullet hole in the drivers door, the round had exited through the passenger door, he said some hunter had done this, from cover, he never saw the person, he went on to give his opinion of careless hunters, what does the reader think of this?, I know I have my own opinion.

Chapter Fourteen

In time the stress, among other things, made me decide to move on, I helped a friend for a while with a small log salvage operation while I planned to leave and travel across the USA, I had no girlfriend to hold me back, my latest gal had just dumped me by the wayside and I was feeling hurt and a little angry toward women in general. my friend George, who no doubt sensed my imminent departure invited me up to his house for coffee, at the same time he invited Frances, now Frances was a friend of his wife's, a deliberate scheme, as anyone can see, he had suggested that I meet Frances many times before, Frances was a pretty girl, still is, (she is my wife now), (but I am getting ahead of myself) but I always said 'thanks, but no thanks; I was determined to leave, nobody was going to foil my plans, but you see The Lord planned otherwise;

Well back to George's house, apparently George's wife had been suggesting to poor Frances that she meet me, Frances was not impressed with any schemes of this nature, but she accepted the coffee invitation, imagine the surprise and embarrassment of the poor girl to find me sitting there!!, After the awkward introductions were in place we sat down to visit with equally awkward conversation, then Frances jumped up to leave, she only lived walking distance away, as soon as she was out of the door George and his wife lit into me, calling me a coward among other unprintable things, now that really hurt, then, a knock at the door, Frances in her hurry to escape had left her purse behind, now, not wishing to be labelled a coward for the rest of my life I asked if I could walk her home, she accepted, very reluctantly I am sure, I walked beside her, up the lane to the door of her house with no further ceremony, said 'Goodnight; and left for home after calling upon mine host to say "Goodnight, and thanks for the setup, it didn't work". I should also say at this point that had she not left her purse behind the whole 'road' might have taken a different turn in my life..

Now I sat at home and thought it all over, I really liked this quiet slim girl, she did not talk very much, and hey!, why not take her out for a coffee, that is if she would go out after our initial poor start, I had no intentions of it going any further than that, I was still determined to travel. Well, she accepted the invitation, we sat quietly in a little cafe in Mission, I was really captivated, I met her family, so different from my reserved English upbringing, they were from Saskatchewan originally, a family of ten, no more of this "how do you do?", handshake stuff, now it was a big hug at the door, 'Come on in have a coffee, sit down, visit a while', scenario.

I found this a little uncomfortable at first, we didn't even hug each other in our own 'Very British" family, but in time, as I fell deeper and deeper into that strange, unexplainable condition known as love, these people were my family now, Dad, as I began to call him did not approve of me at the onset, at least not when he realized that I was getting pretty serious about his daughter, he would get quite irritated by my practice of turning out the porchlight when I would bring Frances home, I would twist the bulb just a little to the left until it went out, he would turn it back to the right the next day when it failed to light.

Anyway despite all this Wilfred Remple became the Dad that I had last seen when I was about seven years old. I am quite sure the family knew that we would get married, I believe that my new "Mom" was happier about this than Dad however. My own Mother really approved of her also. Frances's family probably could not afford to give us a wedding, there were five other children at home, Frances came from a family of ten... One Sunday we packed our stuff and headed for Cour'delene, Idaho, One of the older married sisters, Faye, invited Mom and Dad out for lunch so that we could leave without a scene, a cowardly escape perhaps but better than an argument, Mom knew what we had planned but then she was not opposed to our marriage. It was not the marriage scenario that most young girls dream of, I am sure.

We arrived at "The hitching Post", as the marriage chapel is called, found the Justice of the Peace, dragged in some witnesses off the street and we were man and wife.. I can recall the Four Star motel where we stayed the following night, the hostess was so gracious when she learned that we were newlyweds, we were so terribly 'broke', she gave us a special rate of four dollars for the night, a local bakery supplied a little wedding cake free and we set out on our new life together, as we will always be, as I write I would like to inform the reader that yesterday, the eighteenth of Jan, 2019, was our 54th wedding anniversary, but then I am far ahead in my story and the best is yet to come.

As we returned home I had some misgivings upon how I would be accepted, would Dad be furious that we had actually run away to get married, Mom and Dad could not afford to give us a ceremony, we realized this, now as I approached the door with the brave little light bulb overhead I expected either a cool reception or a punch on the nose, I hoped it would not be the latter.. The door opened, Dad said "Welcome to the tribe, son!" and held out his hand. I soon found out that my new wife and her family were believers in Christ.

I had little or no idea of what she was talking about of course, previously to our actually getting married she had phoned and asked me to watch Billy Graham on TV, I was not particularly interested in Mr Graham, or what he might have to say, after all I was busy in the garden, oh well, I promised to watch, it's amazing that a little girl can accomplish things impossible to Alexander the Great and his army, I was really quite impressed, but I suppose not quite ready to see the truth at the moment., God had that ready for me further down the road.

You see my exposure to Christianity had been at a much younger age, back in Boxford, in the south of England. My sister dragged and my mother pushed this unwilling subject to church and Sunday school to the great stone church in the village, I would sit as the sermon droned on, flies were buzzing in the huge stained glass windows, I had not the slightest idea what was said, only in my mind's eye the river Lambourne flowed peacefully on it's way through the watermeadows only a few hundred yards away, the yellow flag Iris in the meadow, the large trout and grayling lazily swaying in the clear chalk stream water as they waited for a fly to drift by. Then the vicar would give the blessing and I was jolted back to reality and I could make good my escape.

Chapter Fifteen

To return to my wife's request, back here in Canada, I began to realize than perhaps God was not quite so remote and unreachable as previously supposed. We now had an opportunity to travel up into the West Kootenays to a place called Meadow creek, the big Hydro dams were being built, much money was to be made and my wife and I needed a healthy infusion of cash as we started out in life..

We left Mom to look after our house in Chilliwack, Frances's family owned some land and a little cabin identical to the Beverly Hillbillies little house back in the hills in the well known TV series, we fixed it all up inside until it was really cute, I was hired on the dam almost the day that we arrived, working underground on the night shift, not the best setting for the newly weds, I worked seven days a week, no choice. Frances cooked meals and battled the great hordes of mosquitoes, they were out for blood, literally, we scrounged fly screen in an area where one had to travel to Nelson, our nearest real town, forty miles away, in order to buy anything other than the bare necessities of life. The road wound along a mountainside in places where there was only a sheer drop down to the lake below, needless to say it was a whole days adventure to go to town on a shopping trip. I did not know at that point that I would be ploughing snow on that road for the Dept of Highways one day in the future, but there, I am ahead of my story again...

Frances was great, most young women would have gone home to mother at this point and left their lunatic husband behind.. We did make a point of returning to Chilliwack whenever possible, be it only a flying trip, to visit mom and to keep our sanity,.. Now I was about to meet The Lord in a personal way... My wife and I would leave the workplace at the end of a friday shift, whenever I could manage a couple of days off, head out for Chilliwack as fast as our 1957 Turnpike cruiser would travel, it made the 350 or so miles in record time, we would stop at a halfway point and phone to say that we were coming in, Mom was always so happy to see us, she was lonely, her second marriage having been a disaster, she would have the teapot all ready, and was looking forward to the birth of her first grandchild, upon reflection I suppose I should not have been driving as fast as I did in those days. I have heard the expression "never drive faster than your Guardian Angel can fly", our Guardian Angel managed to keep us safe and sound in those early years however.

Chapter Sixteen

Mom developed a really bad hacking cough, she would not see a doctor, for reasons we found out later. She did not answer the phone that particular night, we were not too worried, perhaps she was sleeping. We arrived at a dark quiet house, no lights and no Mother, now we were really worried, just as we considered phoning the police, a neighbour came to the door, she was a good friend of ours, and kept a watchful eye on Mom, she said,' Your Mom was taken sick and I had her admitted to the hospital, the doctor diagnosed it as pleurisy, but not to worry, she is resting comfortably'. We decided it not a good idea to phone the hospital at 11-30 pm, so we would go down in the morning, we were rather relieved because now she would get treatment for that cough at last..

I will remember the next day for the rest of my life, we asked at the desk for Mrs Troy, she kept her second husband's name, she was in intensive care, in an oxygen tent, as white as a sheet, her breath was coming in laboured gasps, as I remembered once watching a dog, run over on the highway, straining for breath, just before it died. The doctor came in and said 'Bill could we talk in my office?'..

Now the terrible cold feeling of dread came over me. He said 'Your mother came in yesterday with what was initially diagnosed as a lung disorder, we had xrays taken, and well, you are an adult, I will have to tell you the worst, her lungs are full of cancer, all her vital organs are cancerous, she can not draw a breath on her own, the oxygen tent is keeping her alive, I can give her a week, maybe two at the most, I'm so sorry Bill!".;.. He went on to say he could not understand her failure to come in at the first sign of trouble, she had after all been a nurse back in England.. sometimes we do not understand the sacrifice that a loving parent gives, concealing the truth so that her children do not have to worry, I did not hear too much else of what Dr Young said that day.. I had heard enough..

We left the hospital, I took Frances back to the house then I had to get away by myself --, suddenly everything came tumbling down around me, nothing was real, even the ground beneath my feet seemed unreal, I thought to myself, how unfair, Mom was looking forward to the birth of our child, only perhaps two weeks away, and now she won't even see the child that she has been busily knitting things for, Mom loved to knit.. I drove up into an old graveyard east of town and sat on a bench under a big maple tree,.. then the tears came, and I really cried, tears did not come easily to this Englishman, we were told that it was a sign of weakness, man was unable to help Mom, and again it was all so unfair, so if the doctor could not help that left only God., that remote God that I hardly had any time for, or even really cared about--

I really prayed sincerely for the first time in my life,' Oh God if you are out there somewhere then please help my Mom, please heal her, give her 18 months at least so that she can see our baby, "I don't really know why I asked for 18 months, only that I did,.. Then the strangest thing, no voice, no audible answer, but a very unusual feeling of peace, nothing that I could generate on my own considering my frame of mind a few minutes earlier. Inside my own self it were as though I heard a voice say "Very well she will be healed;"

I left the graveyard and returned to the house, strangely enough in a much better frame of mind than when I left, I do not remember if I discussed this at length with Frances but the next day I had to get back to work... Up in the

West Kootenay just out of Kaslo is the little community of Meadow Creek, almost next door to the Duncan Dam where I worked,.. A fine Christian gentleman, Mr Bill Kerby, was the Pastor in the church that he had literally built with his own hands and his own money, there are few people of that calibre in the world today.. Frances made me promise to call on him when I returned and he would explain a few things to me,. Well of course I promised with more enthusiasm than I had on my earlier promise to watch Billy Graham.. At this time I had to leave my wife behind to look after the house and to send reports on Mother.

As promised I called on Mr Kerby at the Meadow Creek chapel, he explained God's plan of salvation to me, how He had sent His only Son to die on the cross for my sins, yes I had heard this before, way back in the old church in England, but I had been led to believe that it was an automatic thing, that 'He died to save us all', as the old song', There is a green hill, far away, "implied, we would sing this hymn in school before the misguided "powers that be", had the Bible banned from the schoolrooms of the nation, I did not realize that I had to accept Him as my personal Lord and Saviour, and to ask Him to forgive my sins and to take me just the way I am...

There are many people out there in this world who think that they are beyond forgiveness, they think that they have crossed some invisible line where God will just throw them into the trash can, don't you ever believe it, it's the lie of the enemy, I had done many things in my life of which I am not at all proud, I did not consider myself a sinner, a few lies here and there, borrowed a couple of things, never to return them, but I was just as much in need of salvation as the worst sinner on the planet. God sees us all on the same level, and the most amazing thing is He still loves us and wants us to return to Him. He has promised to cast our sins away just as far as the East is from the West, and most importantly, to remember them no more..

To return to the little chapel, I accepted Christ, repented of my sins and told Bill Kerby about Moms condition, he promised to go and see her at once. In the meantime Frances called with some pretty amazing news, two days after I had left, Mom sat up in the oxygen tent and asked for some food, the nurse brought her some ice cream which she devoured, then she wanted more food, this of course soon caught the attention of Dr Young, our family physician, she was taken back to the xray room for a further exam, and there it was, no cancer detected, I repeat, no cancer, in fact the only abnormality was a slightly swollen arm, there was no previous mistake in diagnosis, the extent of the disease was simply too huge and widespread..

They kept Mom for a few more days for observation, this was simply too crazy for them to accept. Bill Kerby then arrived at the hospital, Mom told my wife at a later date that as he came through the door there was a bright glow or halo around Bill, this scared Mom, she thought at the time that an immortal being had come for her, we all want to go to heaven but are often a little reluctant to die, any way she was then glad to see him arrive.

Bill explained to Mom, as he had to me, the plan of salvation, Mom was by no means an unbeliever or agnostic, she had much the same ideas as myself, in the past, Mom was a good kind person who would help anybody in need, she had an expression that she could never give away her last dollar, it would always be replaced, she would use the expression to 'Cast one's bread upon the water, and it will always return; she felt no more in need of salvation than had I, we never discussed things pertaining to our then far distant God, I had been baptised, or more correctly, sprinkled, in the tradition of the church in England and as far as we were concerned, we were sealed and delivered..

Neither one of us ever went to church in my memory, except perhaps at Easter, apart from my unwilling Sunday visits as a child, previously alluded to, and I should hasten to add that the act of going to church, any church, does not guarantee one's salvation, the main benefit to be gained is to associate with fellow believers, find a good spirit filled Bible believing church that teaches from the Book of life, not somebody else's interpretation of Scripture. But first, make sure that you know the Lord. He will guide you where to go.

Mom was soon discharged, my wife was cooking the meals at home, and keeping me informed, Mom was eating like the proverbial horse, and of all things mowing the lawn, the Doctor was quite baffled by it all, I told him later that I had prayed, he said 'You must have, it was nothing that I could have done'. The case is still on file I am sure with the medical or the cancer foundation, under Troy... Violet Muriel.

Chapter Seventeen

Well the next big event in our lives was the birth of our son, Curt, christened Curtis William, he is known simply as Curt, Mom enjoyed the company of the grandson whom she was not supposed to see, knitting and more knitting, it's funny how English people love to knit, Mom never bought socks, everything was knitted, real wool also, not the synthetic stuff that we pull over our tootsies now, but nice warm fuzzy socks.

To fast forward about 42 years, Curt is now hoping to embark on a missionary ministry together with his wife Toni, he has a wonderful singing voice, and loves 'country Gospel; At the moment he is lay pastor of a small church in Salmo BC. But let's return to our story, sometimes I get 'carried away 'so to speak. I kept at my job working in the Hydro tunnel, underground, Frances stayed home for now and looked after Mom, I had a different feeling toward other people, there again it's hard to describe, a more tolerant feeling, a feeling of concern for others, I think it may be the thing described in the Bible as 'Love', not the mushy, bordering on sexy stuff of Hollywood, which is really 'lust', but the desire to overlook the faults of others and help where help is needed, or asked. I would like to describe some of the events of my life and let the reader form their own opinions, whether "luck", or guidance.

One day we were working on the entrance spillway of the tunnel, about 100 ft from the entrance, I was levering the heavy three quarter inch rebar, or reinforcing bar (to anyone who has not worked in construction,) so that the welder could fuse them together, we were building a web or framework soon to be covered in a concrete pour, I did not feel at all easy about the tunnel roof overhead, it hung in great ominous looking outcroppings, now I had done this many times before but there was just something about that roof!!... I shared my concerns with my fellow worker, the welder, he had a few colourful four letter words to say, he assured me that the scalers, the crew responsible for checking the rockwork, had checked it over, done their job, now let's do ours!. So we carried on for the next four hours or so, lunchbreak arrived, so we carried our lunch buckets out of the tunnel, out into the sunshine, up away from the tunnel mouth.

We didn't hear the roar, I suppose the sound of the earthmovers up above drowned it out, I only know that when we returned to work thirty minutes later the entire roof had collapsed, all of our work was destroyed, huge slabs of rock larger than a pickup truck had smashed the steelwork below like so much spaghetti, we would most certainly have been cut into ten by ten inch squares as we were pushed through the steelwork.. We stood and stared in disbelief, my partner finally blurted out "Were we ever lucky to be outside'!. No, not lucky at all!, God's mighty hand held up that roof until we were safely out of the tunnel, not luck, maybee's, co-incidence, or any other explanation, It was not our time to die, God has an appointed time for us all, until then we are safely in His hands, I only hope that my fellow worker gave some thought to Divine intervention, but somehow I doubt it, he mentioned God quite a bit but not in the manner I would have chosen..

The underground work on the Duncan dam had now petered out and rather than work on the surface where both the rate of pay and the risks were lower, I moved on to another Damsite, out of Revelstoke,.. Once again I was underground, I had a very messy, but not especially hard job, I was working the concrete vibrator, a hand held device about the size of a baseball bat, attached to a long hose, this had to be constantly thrown and pulled, thrown and pulled, so that the concrete, pouring down on our heads much of the time was kept level and in all the corners equally, I should add at this point we all wore heavy yellow oilskin suits that we could hose each other down at the end of the shift--young people, planning to leave school early should try this out for a while, I know that I would have studied for fisheries or anything had I been able to look ahead!!.

Now another miracle is in the near future,.. the big 'Jumbo' as it was called was a steel form, about twelve feet in diameter, and I think about forty feet long, imagine a huge pipe and you have the picture, steel rails, similar to a locomotive track are first laid in the tunnel, on crossties of course, the big jumbo form has wheels and an undercarriage similar to a boxcar, it moves on this track and after the concrete is poured, and set, forming the smooth inner surface of the tunnel, it is contracted slightly, then moved along to another section...

There is a crew who's responsibility it is to move and reset the form, and to oil it so that nothing sticks to the surface of the form, I hope that I am not boring the reader with this description, but my purpose will soon reveal itself.

The crew in question had a very bad tempered foreman who would scream and cuss at them a blue streak, they were largely immigrants, good workers but afraid of being fired, this particular day started badly, they were behind schedule, the language was worse than usual and I suspect that some bolts were not secured but rather than face the foreman they were just left in that position. I had no way of knowing this of course as we walked up the tunnel to the job as I had done for so many days or weeks.

Our foreman was a decent fellow, thank the Lord, but now I stopped and said to our crewboss 'This seems like a good day to quit', I just knew that I needed to walk away, some workers get a phobia, it's the tunnel syndrome, but no, I knew it wasn't that, it was that inner consciousness again, that still small voice. The foreman offered to let me exchange jobs with another man on the crew, he would do my job and I would do his, I accepted, after all it would really make them short handed if I walked off, the strange uneasiness in my chest settled down. In my new job I now sat on the top of a really greasy form that sloped off either way so it was important to stay dead centre, so much better than sliding off and landing in the concrete twelve feet below. There was a sound associated with the concrete pump, a steady thump, thump, that one could almost hear in their sleep at night, that's all there was to life, eat sleep, work, ten hour shifts, I missed my wife a lot of course, but the bills had to be paid, if I had my life to live over I would not do this again.

I carefully pulled up the excess hoses and extension cords as the concrete level rose ever so slowly, then, a sudden jolt, something was very wrong, a loud grinding and the big form began to roll sideways, men screaming, a compressor somewhere, roaring, an air hose, broken away from the compressor was slashing back and forth across the tunnel, somewhere below, similar to an unattended garden hose, turned fully on but much more deadly, I looked at the raw rock roof, nothing to hold on to, then I began to slide down, looking down I saw the form rolling up against the rock wall and I was sliding in to the rapidly decreasing space, between the form and the wall, then the lights went out.

Along the side of the form are portholes, these are used by the foremen to check the concrete levels, and closed when the concrete reaches that level, much like a submarine I suppose, one had been left open, right where I was sliding down, I grabbed it with one hand, at that moment another person slid down and grabbed me, now hauling in two desperate people with one hand seems a little far fetched but it was accomplished in a very short time. I saw the foreman coming along the inner gangplank, now tilted at a crazy angle, asked him for his flashlight, he complied, actually all I could see was the approaching beam of light, I looked back out of the porthole, the concrete was a few inches below, the man who replaced me on that one shift, doing my job was several feet down, buried and crushed,.. Now can we say luck or co-incidence?, no of course not, even to this day I think back to this man who died, he died in my place, not willingly, but I know One who did die willingly for me, if I had been the only human on earth He still would have done so, as it was, the little inner voice warned me on my last shift on that particular hydro dam..

The gas welder was brought in to cut a section out of the form, the man's body was in an upward reaching position, he did not stand a chance, he had a family too, they were coming to see him at Christmas, why me Lord? why him and not me?, if it could only have been both of us saved from death that day... I had to return home with a severely wrenched back, compensation kept me through Christmas, very little if anything was reported on the news, I would imagine that the people responsible for setting up the form have their own nightmare to live with..

Now back to the little house in Chilliwack, Frances, Mom and young Curt, and now I had arrived back home for a while,, Mom had been doing well, then one day asked me to take her to the doctor, he had decided that she had some fluid on the chest, nothing major it seemed, I drove her into the hospital on a Wednesday, she handed me her purse and asked if I would pick her up in a day or two. On Thursday Mom took a turn for the worst, we went to visit, she was yellow with jaundice, obvious kidney failure, I gave her a few grapes, she could barely eat, then the next day the phone call that we all dreaded," I am sorry but your Mother has passed away."

At a time like this satan does his very best to bring in fear and doubt, and I was almost fooled, I even had thoughts that Mom never was really healed, perhaps it was all just a natural turn of events, it was probably 'regression' as the medical term used to describe any improvement in a cancer patient where the disease recedes a bitterness began to creep in, doubts began to form as I began to think, well Mom had a chance to see our son and a short time with us, how long, I added it up in my head, wow! eighteen months and two weeks, almost exactly what I had asked for,!! why had I not asked for eighteen years? I recall asking The Lord to take the extra time allotted to Mom off my lifespan ten times, and if He does, that's just fine, I know where I am going. In first Corinthians 2-9, it is written "That things that the eye has not seen, and the ear has not heard, or things that have not entered into the heart of man, God has prepared for those that love Him..

After realising that my prayer had been answered I felt a peace in my heart, it is written "In all things give thanks", not just the obviously beneficial things, sometimes things that seem to be a disaster at the time are clarified later, He can see the end from the beginning. He does not answer all prayers, especially the ones that could be harmful to others unknown to us further down the road, this situation accomplished two things, it brought me to The Lord, and it brought my Mother to The Lord, neither would have happened, at least not in that way, if Mom had not got sick. I know where she is now and we will some day join her,. Never look a seeming disaster in the face and think that all is lost, the enemy of our soul, it is written, satan walks as a roaring lion, seeking whom he may devour.. don't be fooled by the roaring, instead listen for the small still voice, the inner voice in my case, although I know one man in the Kootenays who actually heard the voice of God, I will describe this later in the book.

Chapter Eighteen

I would like to describe a happening of interest, not the obvious intervention of God, but just to show that he is always there, always ready to help.. I decided to try the Peace River dam, in the Hudson Hope area I flew in by plane, assigned a job in the underground as usual. There I was on the "mucking" crew, a nasty sloppy job but it was work, and well paid, normally we would have a coffee break at ten am, but for some reason nobody stopped work, the whole crew seemed to be afraid to even discuss it, they were all new immigrants and spoke in their own language. When I asked the foreman regarding the absence of the coffee wagon, or the lack of a coffee break, he gave me a very strange look, it was after all written into our union agreement, the next morning at ten the coffee wagon appeared in the tunnel, A really big surprise to the whole crew, it was a hard job and they really needed that fifteen minute break.

About two hrs later a fellow in a brand new clean hard hat and dapper clothes to match, also appeared, looked from side to side, fastened his gaze on me and beckoned toward me to come with him and to bring my lunch pail, as we walked in silence, toward the tunnel entrance, I, being not easily intimidated asked if this was a kidnap, he replied "Sort of, perhaps you shouldn't quote your union manual so freely". Well, the mystery deepens, I told him that I was not too worried, I had lots of backing, this only drove him into complete silence.

We climbed into his nice shiny company pickup truck, he drove me out to a building that looked like a grain elevator on a barren hillside, that turned out to be the batch plant where all our concrete was mixed. In a decidedly unfriendly tone of voice he said to get out here and report to a Dee Henderson, he would put me to work. By this time I had decided that the job was history and I might as well catch the next plane out, but why the silence? the big gravel belt was not running, nothing was happening, I wandered around the building to where a number of men were looking gloomily down into a hole in the conveyor belt housing,: What's up?' said I, cheerfully, a state of mind obviously not shared by the others, one old grumpy looking fellow said that this large bearing shaft had jumped its pillow block and the whole plant was shut down, "So put it back in" I said, he looked at me as though I had really just arrived from Mars, he patiently explained that it would take two men to lift it in and there was only barely room for one in the access hole, he would have to wait for machinery, time is of the essence where concrete is concerned 'Ok! no problem, let me have shot at it', said I, after all I had nothing to lose but my dignity, I was probably on my way out anyway, not having yet found the person I was looking for.

It was a big three inch shaft connected to a pulley that looked, at that moment, about the size of the Empire State building, I felt like Sampson attempting to tear down some giant structure, I was a little slimmer in girth than most of the men standing around, I suspect that standing around had brought on this condition in most of them, I was in decent shape physically in those days of long ago, with a groan I lifted the wretched thing into position, dropped it in its cradle, even to my own amazement, I might add, and climbed out of the hole. The old grumpy looking fellow described earlier, with an ear to ear smile now upon his face said "What's you're name boy?', in a very heavy Oklahoma type accent, I explained that I was looking for a D Henderson, who would put me to work, he said 'I'm Henderson, and just follow me', I sure can find a job for you! "This time I was definitely in more benign company than the officious person who had dropped me off here earlier, perhaps after all I would not be taking the next plane out!

I was given probably the best position in the batch plant, I sat on a little stool waiting for a signal from the operator on the floor above, a buzzer would sound and a red light bulb would show, indicating that he needed a sample, I would then take a cement sample from the concrete pouring past my platform, to the cement trucks waiting below, fill a small bucket with the material, upend the bucket as a child making sandcastles and measure the amount of sag, this was called a slump test, next, I would fill the bucket again, and pour it into a container that resembled a pressure cooker, replace the lid and pump a certain amount of air into the gizmo, taking note of both results, writing them down and taking the calculations, called an air test to the operator above, this was only required about every thirty minutes or so, in order to closely monitor the condition of the concrete being sent out to the tunnel, the tunnel that was the scene of my earlier 'kidnap', now I felt like Joseph, the transfer from the tunnel was planned for my harm, not my good, it later turned out that Mr Henderson had little use for unions, it was obviously planned that he would soon get rid of this young upstart, I am sure that The Lord had the machine breakdown arranged to co-incide with my arrival at the plant, and what is more amazing to give me the strength to lift the thing into place, thus endearing me to the plant foreman,

God works in such miraculous ways in behind the scenes, I might add that I had no further reason to complain re any union non-compliance, so all was quiet on the western front! I have learned in life not to fret when man seeks to cause us harm, whether at home or on the jobsite, what was intended for my harm turned out for my good. A footnote that may be of interest to the reader, I was asked, by one of the crew, if I had seen the Dinosaur tracks in the rock?. I went down to where the workers had blasted away the overburden ready to pour concrete on the clean rock, there were the most perfect tracks of the big lizard that a person could wish for, had I been able to obtain plaster of paris I would have made castings, as it was I took photos, many years ago I would have consulted my Julian Huxley books to determine how many millions of years ago these had been left by the big fellow who took six foot strides, now having seen the evidence in the report on the Glenrose Texas deposits where the tracks of the Dinosaur and of man were made in the same rock strata, obviously occurring at the same time in history. Scoffers and unbelievers claimed that the human tracks were inserted at a later date, they stripped back the overburden from the stream bank, and guess what?, the tracks continued uninterrupted under several feet of soil and gravel, that would be a very difficult 'hoax' to say the least, I find that the evolution theory, and theory it can only be, is seriously flawed. The tracks, I might add were quickly covered with concrete and little was said about them, perhaps a news report may have held up the dam, while swarms of experts may have milled around the area. In any case the big Peace River dam is now in place. This would be my last job away from home.

Chapter Nineteen

I worked for a short while in the Chilliwack area once more as I had, and still have a love for the Fraser Valley, down in the Southwest corner of British Columbia. I would like to relate an experience that will be of interest to the reader, something that did not happen to me personally, but it happened to a fellow worker. Malcolm M, he and I worked together on a nearby packing house, I was hauling produce into the USA, and he worked in the plant. We were discussing the events surrounding my Mothers healing, and of course her eventual death, I told him of my beliefs concerning the Lord's constant presence in my life. He then told me of the following amazing experience in HIS life. I will say at this point that Malcolm did not talk too freely about personal matters, so

I considered it a privilege that he shared it with me, often people are reluctant to discuss things that have happened in their lives, unfortunately society as a whole refuse to accept things of a spiritual nature, the attitude seems to be 'If you can't touch it, it does not exist'..

He had been married for a year and his first baby was due, he and his wife were so excited about the arrival of their addition to the family.. the child was born without incident, but the unthinkable happened, the young child was taken sick, grew steadily worse, and died. Malcolm could not be consoled, as he related it to me, he sat in the window of his house, staring outside in absolute misery, he was looking up into the sky when his attention was focused on a small sharp point of light far away, the light grew closer and closer, and also much larger, it came directly to his window, he was clearly embarrassed as he spoke, afraid I am sure that I would laugh, I listened in great interest, he then told me that it assumed the shape of an Angel, right outside the window, I asked at this point if it appeared as a conventional Angel, with wings, he said yes it did. I believe that the Lord will always send His messengers or appear in a way that we will understand.

Malcolm tried to call his wife, words would not come, finally when he could speak, the being had faded away.. his wife came running but clearly this was for Malcolm alone. now the rest of the story--they had another child in due course, a fit and healthy child, the duplicate image of the former baby. I know for certain that he would not have shared this with me had I not told him the amazing story of my Mother, I think it is so sad that people do not share such experiences with each other without the fear of being ridiculed. The foregoing experience that Malcolm had would be a very good reason to belong to a Bible believing church, he never attended church and so he never had a chance to share his story with others.

Chapter Twenty

We decided that it would be a good plan to move back up into the West Kootenay area, the fishing was great, and I love to fish, the Fraser Valley traffic and the slow pollution of the air and water in Chilliwack, once so proud of it's clean air, prompted us to move on. Bill Kerby, (the Pastor from Meadow Creek, the man who led be to The Lord, you will recall), offered us a house with a lake view and frontage on Kootenay Lake, beside the little community named Mirror Lake, after a small lake, or more correctly, pond, in the small cluster of houses, we realised a good price for our Chilliwack property, Bill gave us a deal that we could not refuse,.. the house had it's own 100 feet of lakeshore on what is probably one of the remaining unpolluted fresh water lakes in the Province of BC.

We loved to fish and there were lake trout and kokanee in abundance, firewood to cut, backroads to explore, a natural hotspring to visit in nearby Ainsworth, it was a great place to live and raise our son, he loved to fish just as much as his Dad, we had a small non denominational church nearby, all was well in paradise, the only drawback perhaps the heavy snow in the winter, but even snow has value, it contains nitrogen in minute quantities and has been called 'The poor man's fertilizer', what else keeps the forests green, and the rivers flowing? what else could form the perfect insulated blanket for plant life against bitter cold?

As we get older we ponder the wonders of God's creation, nothing is 'accidental' in nature, only when man tampers with the balance by introducing animals or plants outside their natural habitat, in his wild desire to tag, weigh, compute, study, re-locate, and otherwise mess with a system that no human brain could have devised --do things go wrong. I would like to take the reader back to the south of England, to my beloved water meadows, I attended the little schoolhouse where The Lords prayer always started the days activity, the Bible was not banned in those days, evolution was taught, along with the Bible, the student was left with their own choice of direction.

We had a vicar who had a natural explanation for everything, the burning bush for instance was St Elmo's fire, a natural phenomenon in the Everglades, he didn't explain the climate difference between the Florida swamps and the Judain desert. Anyway... the parting of the Red Sea he claimed was simply brought about by a great wind, amazing how this wind could blow in two directions at once, somehow I failed to see how this man could be doing God's work, even if He was, at that time, a far distant God, this all took place of course long before I discovered The Lord..

Mom bought some of the best study books of the day, all on the evolution theory, I studied Julian Huxley until I had it all sorted out in my mind, I knew every dinosaur by his first name, but there was still the problem of creation to deal with, for a while I reasoned perhaps God put man on earth using the ape from the tree theory, then why the story of the Garden? For years I tried to work out this problem, if anybody should try to advance the evolution theory to me at least by accusing me of ignorance, then I can safely say that I have read, studied, and discarded..

Let us return to Mirror Lake. By now of course the events in my life, the times when He was there when I needed Him most, all served to verify that I had made the right choice, but again on reflection He chose me before I even knew Him. We now were totally out of debt, the house paid in cash, money over from our Chilliwack sale. We just decided to take it easy for a while and just fish and laze around,.

Chapter Twenty One

At this point I happened to be talking to the foreman of the Highway Dept, which at that time was a branch of the BC Govt, it was something about gathering rocks from the ditch to build a rock wall at home, he said "By all means, take plenty, take them all!!.. We talked awhile, small talk about our moving to the area, he asked if I would be interested in a back road clearing project up the South Fork road as it was called, this narrow gravel road culminated at the foot of a glacier, at the Kootenay campground, it was a steady climb, Well I owned a chainsaw, it was contract, nothing to tie me down, why not? use of the Govt pickup truck to boot!, even in paradise I was getting a little bored. It was fun, not easy work, the other man involved and myself made good progress, and good money, we were paid by the footage cleared,

..It was later in the year, we had not reached our destination of the Kootenay Glacier at the headwaters of the South Fork creek that ran alongside the road, the snow began to fall and we brought our work to a close... Ah! now to return to the lazy life. The foreman asked if I would like to stay on and do some snow removal,? well ok,! I had a vision of clearing of bridges with a shovel now and then, but no, this involved getting a higher class licence, an air ticket, and being presented with an ugly yellow snowplough truck to drive, Help!, well, what else would I do during the winter except survey the very deep snow we had in that area out of the window?? It always seemed as though work followed me around, always waiting to spring from the shadows. At least I always did my best, in whatever I did,.. the roads were very treacherous in that area, in fact they have not changed too much to this day, Coffee Creek bluff is simply a narrow road cut into a cliff face, part of the main road between Nelson and Meadow Creek, up above the road is a sheer cliff, with rockslides and snowslides, depending on the season, below it plunges straight down into Kootenay lake, several hundred feet below. A beautiful unspoiled area to visit in summer, but an area for extreme caution in winter.

That invitation to clear snow turned into a regular full time job for the next seven years, I stayed on with the Ministry of Highways, ploughing snow in winter, maintaining roads in summer, hauling rock and gravel, patching potholes and other fun jobs! Now The Lord was about to come to my rescue again. A small fleet of our trucks were repairing a washed out section of road to the north of Meadow creek, the river was in full flood mode, coming down from the glaciers far upstream in an icy blue-green flood. It had undercut the gravel road so that only one and one half vehicle widths remained in some areas, it was a narrow and winding road, with tall evergreens alongside, so that our trucks were not visible to each other most of the time, we used our radios to keep track of each others position and avoid nasty surprises, we could also locate and report private vehicles to ensure their safety.

Loads of rock, called "Rip rap" were going up to the worst areas, to stem the rivers advance and of course the empty trucks were coming down. I was heading up with a load of rock, as I was going into a blind spot, where the road was very narrow and undercut I called "Up at thirty one" translated of course that means I'm coming up at thirty one mile, at once the call came back, "down at thirty one", meaning of course that an empty truck was right around the next corner. The empty always made way for the loaded, and sure enough around the next corner was my partner

John, he had squeezed his truck in as far as possible to the bank on the upper side of the road, leaving me with room to slowly drive through, the problem being that the road was severely undercut at this point, the reader might ask why did we not repair the sections that we were driving over first,? I have no answer to that!!, I believe that I stated earlier that this was a Provincial Govt project. As my heavily loaded truck squeezed through I felt the road beneath buckle and shift, the truck rolled into the Lardeau River, I took one deep breath as the water poured in through the side vents, hitting me with the force of a fire hose, then a cold dark greenish silence as I struggled to escape, the vehicle was now totally upside down in the river, the gear shift now comes down from above, I tried to unfasten my seat belt, instead I was pulling on my pants belt buckle, I would like to say that I called on The Lord but I would be lying, I was scared, very scared, I was bursting for air, then a strange 'inner' unheard voice seemed to say "Drowning is an easy death, just take a deep breath and it's all over" The voice of the enemy of our souls was talking to me in my inner being. It is written that satan stalks around as a roaring lion, seeking who he may devour, I have read reports from hunters in Africa, the lion roars to intimidate and strike fear into it's intended victims, it certainly had that effect upon me at that moment in time- -but-- My Lord and Saviour had other plans that day, it was not my time to die..

The river is glacier fed, it was very cold, then I found the seat belt latch, at least now I could get out, but the drivers door was jammed, I crossed the cab somehow, crawling through the gearshift, and tried the passenger door, it opened, I climbed up the side of the truck and stuck my head out into God's clean air, a person has no idea how wonderful the sight of trees and blue sky can be without such an experience, it has been said that to really live, one must almost die, I can relate to that, I said "Praise The Lord "several times as I gulped some sorely needed air. My friend John had radio'ed in a "Mayday, truck in the river', as he watched it all in front of his eyes, he stood on the bank watching the bubbles rise from the submerged cab, hoping that I would soon emerge, he said later that he did not know what to do, but there was little he could do, the river was very swift and deep, if Johnny reads this then may God bless him, I will always love him as a brother and he will always be my friend..

The foreman gave me the pickup truck to transport my soaking wet, very grateful to God, self, home.. they pulled the truck out of the river, using a grader for the task, it turned out later that a huge boulder, dislodged by the river, and my descending truck, had been precariously balanced alongside the door from which I had escaped, it had to be winched out first in order to avoid possible further injury to the truck, had this great rock slipped against the door then it would have been more difficult, if not impossible to exit the cab.

That same great Angel that held up the tunnel roof was there to hold back the boulder. Some might say' Why did you not roll down a window,? I would like to say here that when you are upside down in a vehicle in the water, unable to breath, unable even to see, rational thoughts do not come easily, the enemy of our soul waits for moments like these. The dump truck I should add, suffered little harm apart from a broken mirror and a dent or two. landing in the water cushioned it's fall I would imagine. To this day a neat mound of rock marks the spot in the river,

Two weeks later it was out of the repair bay and I was driving it once more. The question some might ask at this point may well be 'What do you think of seat belts',? in view of the fact that it was so difficult to release? this question was put to me at the enquiry where I was thankfully exonerated from blame in this whole affair, my answer here as back then,' I believe that without the seat belt I may well have struck my head on some object in the cab, rendered unconscious or even partly so, then drowning would have been the end result'. I do thoroughly believe in the use of seat belts, to me, after driving for many years, to click on the belt is as automatic as releasing the park brake, of course God is able to save us from our own foolish actions, but I don't think as believers that we should put God to the test, it is written that we are able to pick up any deadly thing, or drink any deadly substance and it will not harm us, I don't think for a moment that we should pick up rattlesnakes to test God, this does not honour God, if we do our part then He will protect us!!.

In my earlier years I swam in Cultus Lake, in the Fraser Valley, I liked to swim underwater, in the partitioned off areas, searching the bottom for watches, rings or any lost items, wearing goggles of course that I might see clearly, I learned to hold my breath for extended periods, and I often wonder if this had helped me in the truck incident later in life? I have an amusing, {at least to any bystanders], incident to relate,, I owned a Peterborough seventeen foot canoe back when I was single and foolish, living in Chilliwack, it was a traditional canvas covered thing of beauty, so stable that I could tip the gunwale down to water level, always paddling on one side of course, as a person is supposed to do, I even crossed the Fraser River several times, with no flotation device aboard, well, I did say that I was foolish!! My Angel has always been very busy.. While living at Mirror Lake years later, I bought a sixteen foot fiberglass canoe, one day I took it out on the lake to demonstrate to my son how to paddle with the water at gunwale level, only the craft did not stop at the intended level, it kept rolling and dumped me in the lake, my son was quite amused at least! It's very hard to beat the canvas covered cedar for stability.

To return to the truck driving routine for the Ministry.. I could have carried on into retirement, living at our lakeshore 'resort', we owned a nice 19 foot cabin cruiser, did a little fishing in the lake, had the best neighbors one could wish for living behind us, Jim and Sadie, fellow believers, Jim had an amazing experience with the Lord, he is the only man I know who has actually heard the voice of God, I will relate it as he explained it to my wife and myself, here again, I am writing down the experience of someone other than myself, but I do know without any shadow of a doubt that this man speaks the truth.

He was cutting down a big tree, with a chainsaw taking all the necessary precautions, when a voice said "Step back", he questioned the voice, answered, "What?", again the voice, louder now, "Step back "so Jim stepped back and a big tree limb crashed down, right where he had been standing a moment before, in the logging industry this is known as a 'Widowmaker', with good or should I say grim reason.. God sometimes uses a small inner voice, as in my case, sometimes an audible unmistakeable voice, as in Jim's, in any case be sure that you are always "tuned in' to the voice of God.

Chapter Twenty Two

Frances and I were growing restless, it's hard to explain, some people can live in the same town all their lives and be content, it may have been the long trip to Nelson for groceries and necessities that took one whole day to accomplish, it may have been a feeling of being hemmed in by the beautiful snow capped peaks of the mountains around us, or a combination of such things, I think it was probably an urging of the Lord to move on, He had other things to show us. We had been drawn to the Okanagan Valley by the numerous times we had driven through on our trips back and forth to the Kootenays, the sun always seemed to be shining and smiling upon this land of brown hills and lush orchards, we would pick up fresh fruit from the many farmer owned fruit stands that line the highway on either side of the Towns of Oliver and Osoyoos as we passed through.

The thought increasingly entered our minds' Why not move here, why not buy our own little orchard? Now the idea of an orchard or farm of any kind did not appeal to Frances, to move here was fine, but a normal house on a normal street please, no orchard. Well my son Curt was all for the farm idea, he loved animals, and of course we still do, he had visions of rabbit hutches and a place for his beloved dog, Dan, to run, so in spite of my wife's misgivings, we bought a small four acre orchard in the rural area of Oliver. The real estate agent painted a rosy picture of the orchardist's life, and of course I was all ears, as the saying goes and just lapped it up.

During the fall and winter the farmer did his pruning, and some fall spraying, then he would take his profits and seek a warmer climate for a well needed rest, returning in spring to complete the pruning and spraying before harvest time rolled around again, thus his self employed life, disregarding all alarm clocks and worldly time schedules rolled on, kept busy of course by mowing between the trees with the tractor drawn mower at intervals. Now this was the life. Several things were omitted from the picture, first one had to own at least ten acres to make any kind of a living, next, and I think the most important the farmer has to spray almost continually for various pests and diseases, some real, and some 'preventitive', with a bewildering assortment of the most horrible chemicals known to mankind outside of a war zone.

Now I would have preferred to use an 'organic 'approach, but in an area where all the neighborhood orchards were using chemicals, as previously described, where both the pest and the natural predator of the pest were slain in the same fell swoop, it would not work. Now in these later days, I am happy to report, much study has been done, many of the chemicals have been outlawed, and many farmers are using the organic approach, and I might add, getting a better return for their crops, not to mention the health of the customer. We even have a 'Sterile insect release' program, where sterilised Codling moths are released into the orchards, this is the well known and despised 'Apple worm' in its juvenile state, they meet up with natural moths and attempt reproduction, the poor little guys don't know that they have picked a dud and so the species is diminished, hopefully one day, wiped out, the only fly in the ointment, or orchard, pardon the pun!, is the fact that the orchards in that area roll on down to, and beyond, the US border, often only a wire fence marks the boundary between the two countries, we lived only about the distance of one half mile from the USA, if they do not have a similar program in force then they will gleefully meet up with their US cousins... no passport required!!

Well here we were, green as grass, the picture of naive natives in an unknown situation, faced with the problem of selling our fruit that was rapidly ripening on the trees, in order to meet a mortgage payment just ahead. Yes, your are so right! I should have listened to my wife, we had received enough for our Kootenay property to have purchased a normal little house on a street in town, but not enough to buy even a small orchard outright. We picked and picked until we were as brown as the surrounding hills, peaches, apples, cherries, prune plums, nectarines, all picked as they ripened, carefully packed in boxes, some hauled back up into the Kootenays, some I would sell from the back tailgate of our truck, positioned at a wide spot on the highway. They were free from spray and The Lord gave us good crops, no pests or disease apparent, we had tons and tons of apples, the farmers were getting next to nothing for them so we literally shovelled them into bins and hauled them to the juice plant, to render down for apple juice, we actually received almost as much as the carefully picked and tended crops that the local orchardists were hauling to the packing house, in fact in many cases the farmer received a bill for handling from the packinghouse, instead of a cheque, yes incredible I know but such is the life of a farmer in many instances.

Well our Lord bailed us out, we sold all the fruit, made the mortgage payment and put the orchard up for sale, a young couple bought it, we realised our original price, so a lesson was learned in the process. Houses on the market were few and far between, our next venture was an eight acre field with a house and an old barn, loosely described as a farm, now Curt was happy, he set up his rabbit hutches, and the faithful dog Dan had room to run, I went back to the local Highway dept as winter relief, we bought a horse for Curt, a wild unbroken half Arab, probably not the best choice. We planted a large patch of strawberries, Frances sold the fruit in spring, encouraged by our success we planted one half acre, I was laid off from highways in the springtime so we planted more strawberries, soon we became a strawberry farm, this was to become our major source of income for the next couple of years.

We sold the horse when Curt discovered girls, they were more fun it seemed. I was developing a really sore hip,, strawberries grow very close to the ground, between weeding and dragging irrigation pipes around it was causing a problem,. I returned to the Highway dept on a full time basis, the large amount of driving was more restful to the old hip. Curt had graduated from school and returned to the Kootenays to work.

..About this time a real estate agent with who'm I had a good friendly relationship, and who also understood our desire to sell the farm, came to me and said "Bill, do I have a deal for you!" oh sure, I had heard that line somewhere before, nevertheless I thought it worth checking out, he took me out to this cute little house along the highway, about one half mile or less from the US border, now without consulting each other, Franny has this gift of discernment, remember the orchard?, we just knew that this was our house, it was not to be listed until the following morning, the price was astoundingly low, as we walked in we needed no sales pitch to convince us,

One of the things that I have learned in life is that The Lord is always on hand if we listen to the still small voice within.. I gave a cheque to the agent on the spot, as a down payment to hold the property, we just knew that this was the place for us, it was on a sloping half acre lot only three miles from town. Osoyoos is located, geographicly speaking at the northern tip of the Great Sonoran Desert, we were in a 'rain shadow' receiving very little rainfall, and much sunshine, the farm sold later and here we were, finally in the "house on the street' that Frances had dreamed of. It was a 'friendly' house, very difficult to explain, have you ever walked into a house that 'repelled' you or made you feel uneasy? On the other hand some houses seem to say 'Welcome, come on in!'.

We had small cacti, not so small rattlesnakes,[though I am pleased to announce they keep mainly away from human habitation], (Frances hates snakes of any description) even a few small scorpions if one looks under rocks on hot days, here again they are out in the 'wasteland', and best left alone. We had the warmest freshwater lake in Canada, according to the Chamber of Commerce, the valley itself is simply beautiful, many people come in winter to experience our relatively mild climate and absence of snow, here again sometimes we get a little more than the 'corn broom' clearing two inches or so, many come from Alberta and Saskatchewan to escape the howling blizzards of their home territory.

Chapter Twenty Three

The next few years passed with little out of the ordinary, my son married a local girl and took her back into the Kootenays, it turned out to be a match not "made in heaven", a fact that gave my wife and I much sorrow.. they had a baby girl before their divorce, (Rebecca was 16 years old at the time of writing, and a very pretty young lady, how the time flies!)

Curt returned to the Kootenays alone, where he forsook The Lord and my wife's Christian upbringing. He was bitter and hurt, but... It is written "Bring up a child in the way he should go, and when he is old, he will not depart from it". The Lord is gracious and kind. He heard the prayers of Fran and I. Curt met Toni, a girl who also had experienced a really rough life, she also had two children from a bad marriage.. Toni was not a believer when she met Curt, but as she said later, there was something about this quiet man that she had never experienced before, quite frankly Frances and I were worried, who was this strange woman keeping company with our son?.. Well they fell in love and were married. The Lord of all definately had it in His Plan, now Toni and Curt have a ministry together that only God could have orchestrated, Curt sings with a testimoney and Toni backs him up with her life story, when they minister upon invitation the whole place is hushed, there is an "electrical" feeling as the Spirit moves.

The Lord has given Curt a magnificent voice, they had a child together,. Will is now a fine young man of sixteen at the time of writing. My sister Joan thinks that Curt should have studied for opera!? He is not remotely interested in opera, they are hoping to buy a bus one day when it's in God's timing, and they will travel this land telling how no matter how low you think you have sunk, The Lord forgives all if we only confess our sins to Him. But that will be a story that only Curt and Toni have the right to tell. Once they have the finances to buy the bus, and they will. God will work a miracle in their lives, and it is always in some un-dreamed of, un-imagined fashion that the Lord does his work, at least that has been my experience, God will cause something to happen, of one thing I am sure, when He moves, He lets it be known that it is in His timing.!

As a backnote to this chapter, Curt and Toni have bought their bus, a forty foot diesel pusher and named it 'Faith', a very apt title I might add!

Chapter Twenty Four

My hip gave more trouble until the highway foreman told me in no uncertain terms that I must take a disability leave, he watched me climb out of the truck at the end of the shift and hobble into the shop to sign off for the day,, now I do believe that The Lord heals, it is written "By His stripes we are healed" not could be, or may be, but are healed, now I had seen this miracle of healing with my Mother, much earlier in this book, and I believe that it is as much for today as when Christ was on earth, it is written: The Lord changes not" and I believe that, however, that said, also I believe that He does it in his timing, not ours, and often he wants to show us something more..

I scheduled a hip replacement and waited almost a full year before the surgery could take place. We decided that the sloping lot was too hard to maintain so we thought it would be better to buy into a Strata complex. We sold our little house near the border, I thought at the time that it was a mistake, but God allows us to make mistakes, we allow our children to make mistakes, provided they are not serious ones,, and so they learn, The Father is no different with His children, in fact I believe that we could understand Him better if we cast ourselves in the same relationship with a total dependence upon Him, after all is said and done, we can not take our next breath without Him!.

We moved into our little Strata house, I felt very restricted with the tiny lot, but did as much gardening as possible, old gardeners never die, they just turn to compost, I wonder if Shakespeare said that? but no matter. I checked into the Penticton Hospital for the awaited operation, the next day found me on the operating table, given a spinal, and presumably waiting for the final anaesthetic before the surgery began, the technician talked to me about various subjects as I laid there, this is usually done to test a patients conscious state of mind to see when they are ready to "go under", however I was bright and cheerful, it was then that I heard this sawing sound, and the table was moving up and down. Apparently they were sawing off the delinquent hip, and I could not feel a thing, I was totally without any feeling from the waist down, I asked to see the part they had removed and he held up this thing reminiscent of a dog bone, I wanted to keep it but "No, sorry sir you can not take this home to preserve in alcohol." The steel replacement was installed and I was wheeled into the recovery room.. The surgeon did an excellent job, I felt like an old car with a rusted out cab mount now replaced.

Three days later I walked up and down in front of the nurses station holding my walker up in the air, the message I was trying to impart was that I would do so much better and recover so much quicker with my wife's excellent cooking, as opposed to the hospital fare, strange thing about hospital food, it all tastes the same even when the menu is changed, I suspect the reason for the little slip of paper residing on the plate, is so that a person can accurately identify the food according to colour and /or shape. The doctor gave me the high sign to return to my dear wife and delicious food, she sometimes asks if this is the reason that I married her [of course not, what a preposterous idea,]! But then the old adage "The way to a man's heart is through his stomach" was probably coined by a man with a wife like mine perhaps we should leave this subject right here!!.

..Soon after returning home I had a dream, I know that it was from The Lord because it helped me endure some very bad times just ahead... The healing of my hip progressed rapidly, soon I was walking with the aid of a stick, no pain, no discomfort. One night I dreamed that I was in a battle, I had a rifle and the enemy were coming up fast, I was shooting the enemy soldiers in the head and they were going down rapidly, soon the battle was won and I heard a voice say distinctly, "The battle of San Jacinto' I woke up with these words still strongly in my mind, and I wrote them down at once. The next day I mentioned this to my daughter in law, Toni and she searched the "Web' for an answer, we did not own a computor at that time, up came the info requested,. Sam Houston led the battle against the forces of Santa Anna along the San Jacinto river in the State of Texas on the 21st of April, 1836, here is the best part, across the screen, flashed a 'Banner', as Toni described it, saying 'Jesus is Lord, Victory is certain!". Victory as we all know, also blessed Sam Houston on that day so long ago.

Chapter Twenty Five

I was required to attend the nearby physio clinic as part of the healing and recovery program, as Frances and I sat awaiting my turn, Frances said "Let's get out of here!" she had the strong urge just to leave, how I wish in hindsight that I had obeyed that "inner voice; The therapist had me laying on my back while she took my newly repaired leg and moved it up high in the air, I had been instructed by the surgeon and by all the paperwork supplied by the hospital not to move it tighter than 90 degrees, my wife, who was watching this procedure, wondered why I did not complain, well, aren't these people supposed to know what they are doing, and why? Well I felt a definate snap, or click in my hip, it was now quite sore, so we went home.

That night was really bad, much pain and no sleep, the next morning found my wife driving me the twelve miles to Oliver hospital, they could not help, so the ambulance ferried me further to Penticton hospital, they gave me morphine to ease the incredible pain in my leg. In time the pain subsided and I was sent home, I had the strange sensation of something running down my leg, but it was on the inside it would seem, the pain returned, in great agonising waves, the ambulance also returned, and back to the hospital bed I went. Now the doctor diagnosed inner bleeding, my leg was huge and swollen, they fitted me with something akin to a huge milking machine that pulsed away as it drew the blood out of my leg, that gave some relief.

To return for a moment to my dream of the preceding week, I would turn it over and over in my head as I lay in great pain, and the words "Jesus is Lord, Victory is certain" would comfort me as nothing else would. He did not say that we would be immune from pain and suffering, only that He would never leave us or forsake us. One thing that I cannot emphasize strongly enough, when you hear that little voice inside, obey, listen, how I wished in good old hindsight that I had stood up and left that physio clinic.. In time I was discharged, and back home, in far worse shape than three days after the operation, initially the surgeon had done an excellent job, now I was a semi invalid in the care of my poor long suffering wife, I learned later that I had been in danger of losing that leg, but God is good. Recently I heard the expression that God does not guarantee a smooth passage, but He does promise a 'safe landing'...

Of course I needed a shower as soon as I returned, very very carefully I took my shower, I bent over to one side to wash the outside of the leg when, clunk!, with an audible sound something terrible happened, now my right foot faced inward, as though it didn't belong to me, it hung there, I grabbed for the shower curtain, falling out of the shower, taking the curtain, the towel and the towel rail all along with me on my rapid descent to the bathroom floor, Frances heard the great commotion, called out "Are you allright? "a feeble "No" from your hero as I laid half in the tub and half on the floor, she opened the door in a millisecond to help me to my feet, oh yes! and the offending leg was back in place, I stood on it once more it was definately out of the hip socket, how did it return? I am going to leave that to your imagination.. This would disjoint several times after this when I was not careful, but I learned how to return it to it's socket by pressing outward on my knee and inward with the other hand on my hip, it then would make an audible "clunk "again and the good old right foot would return to it's normal stance, straight ahead.

Do not let me discourage anybody from having a hip replaced if really needed, I find that a visit to the dentist is more painful and stressful, my experience was due to the incompetence of the gal in the physio lab, nothing else, I really don't know why The Lord did not heal me in this instance, I prayed for a healing of my hip for months before the operation, perhaps He wanted me to go through this thing to sense His presence I recall Katherine Kulman, the lady who had so many miraculous healings in her ministry, saying that she did not understand why a person, perhaps sitting up front, convinced that they would be healed, were not, whereas a sick but sceptical person back in the audience would receive instant healing. One thing is for sure, we do not order God around, He is omnipotent, He is all seeing, the human mind can not comprehend, can not hope to really understand A Being that was here before time. (I am going to add a footnote at this point, I have had the other hip replaced since the earlier writing and it was a perfect pain free operation, I am now riding my bicycle and walking, completely at ease with my 'aftermarket' hips..)

Try if you will to imagine unending outer space, the wonder of the eye, that camera that records our experiences as we go through life and imprints them indelibly upon the miracle that we call the brain, try to imagine this wonderful planet called Earth, hanging in space with no visible means of support, rotating at exactly the same speed, century in, century out, science assures us that were we just a little closer or a little further from the Sun then life as we know it would be impossible. One thing I would really impress upon the reader in the closing chapter of this book---Be sure that no space exists between you and the Son, the Son of God, who died for you and for me, Many of our scientists are believers, many are not, it is written than God uses the foolish things to confound the wise.

May God richly bless your life as He has mine. My wife Frances, and myself are planning to visit England together, and soon, sixty seven years after the sailing of the M.V. Georgic out of Southampton, England. The poet, I believe that it was Sir Walter Scott, wrote.. "Lies there the man, with soul so dead, who never to himself hath said "This is my own, my native land," who's heart has ne'er within him burned, as home his footsteps he hath turned, from wandering on a foreign strand. Canada is now my home,---but no true'r words than this were ever written.... Footnote from the Author---. As I read this account written some time ago I would like to add that I am now 87 years old, (In September 2019,) my wife Frances and myself have our 50th wedding anniversary behind us now, we are still rejoicing in The Lord,-- He has pulled me through two serious incidents since this book was written- I had a hard fall on the icy street while unloading our vehicle outside a market, apart from a headache I thought little of it until a day or so later I was unable to stand up, the ambulance picked me up at home, the medics were not too optimistic, when I awakened in hospital I was hooked up to a bag, filling with blood, via two tubes to my head, apparently I had a serious blood issue that would have been terminal had it broken through the thin protective layer over the brain, the nurse told me I came very close to death, but there again, The Master knew otherwise--- Second incident some time later, I awoke with a shivering sensation at 3 am one morning, I told Frances to just wait until morning, it got worse, so along came the ambulance again, I would add at this point I was only semi-conscious at the time, it turned out that I was seriously "septis"' we did not recognise the symptoms at the time but the ambulance driver requested the name of next of kin, not the most pleasant experience for my poor wife—Once more, the familiar surroundings of the hospital, apparently the doctor had difficulty identifying the anti-biotic needed, but at the last minute they did, the nurse with her finger indicated that I had come "That close" to death", but once more, The Master decided, "Not just yet" Jesus is Lord, our God is Lord of all, and so I feel the urge to write this book, never give up, when the skies are dark then pray—accept Christ, He died for you and me—As the former story would indicate He did not promise smooth "sailing" in this life, only a safe landing-just listen for that small still voice!—Bill Richens